Aristotle

Dramatics

Aristotle

Dramatics
(also known as *Poetics*)

Commentary and Translation by
Gregory L. Scott

An Emendation of the translation by Ingram
Bywater (1920), with consideration of the Greek
text of L. Tarán and D. Gutas (2012)

ExistencePS Press
New York, NY

ExistencePS Press

Aristotle
Dramatics
(also known as Poetics)

Commentary and Translation by
Gregory L. Scott

Edition 1

Softcover

Copyright © 2020
Gregory L Scott

All rights reserved.

New York, NY
United States of America

ISBN-13: 978-1-952627-00-2

Library of Congress Control Number (LCCN):
2020907216

Dedicated to the memory of

Daniel de Montmollin

1921-2017

who helped guide me through Aristotle's "Poetics"
at the University of Toronto and who was correct
in ways he never imagined.

Aristotle DRAMATICS

Table of Contents

Foreword ix
Acknowledgments x
Updates xiii
Introduction xvii
The Title and Nature of the Book xix
The Core Greek Terms xxii
Single Treatise or Amalgamation? xxx
Catharsis xxxiv
Why not an Original Translation? xxxix
Summary and Principles xlv

DRAMATICS

Chapter 1 1
Chapter 2 4
Chapter 3 5
Chapter 4 7
Chapter 5 11
Chapter 6 13
Chapter 7 17
Chapter 8 19
Chapter 9 20
Chapter 10 23
Chapter 11 23
Chapter 12 26
Chapter 13 27
Chapter 14A 29

CHAPTER 14B 31
CHAPTER 15 34
CHAPTER 16 37
CHAPTER 17 40
CHAPTER 18 42
CHAPTER 19 45
CHAPTER 20 46
CHAPTER 21 51
CHAPTER 22 54
CHAPTER 23 58
CHAPTER 24 60
CHAPTER 25 64
CHAPTER 26 69

Bibliography 73

Introduction

Foreword

This book culminates over 30 years of work that include related publications, starting with my PhD dissertation under Francis Sparshott at the University of Toronto. The translation is unique in that it goes against the previously never-questioned view that Aristotle's extremely influential treatise, which helps form the foundation of Western literary, dramatic, artistic and aesthetic theory, was about literary criticism or the like. Rather, the translation takes it for granted, based on the rigorous arguments already published, that Aristotle focusses on three "musical dramatic" arts—tragedy, comedy and epic—that necessarily also have music, "ordered body movement" or dance (gestures in the case of the singing epic rhapsode) and, in the case of tragedy and comedy, spectacle with actors acting.

The book also takes a stance that is still anathema to many of the scholars specializing in Platonic and Aristotelian philosophy, namely, that the Northern Greek from Stagira could not have written the word *katharsis* (or indeed the whole catharsis-clause with pity and fear) in the definition of tragedy. I am proud to say, though, that world-renown specialists are increasingly coming to accept and publish support for my view, for reasons explained in my previous publications and summarized in the Introduction.

In effect, the translation presents the Stagirite's theory

in the way originally intended, absolves him of a host of criticisms leveled at him over the ages, especially pertaining to whether his theory could handle newer approaches to literature, and opens new possibilities in Aristotelian aesthetics and its applicability to current and future "musical" drama.

Acknowledgments

Those who have offered encouragement over the years, even if they disagreed on some or many points, are Calvin Normore, D.S. Hutchinson, Brad Inwood, Robert Crease, Ronald Polansky, Paul Woodruff, David Sedley, Alexander Mourelatos, Nickolas Pappas, George Boys-Stones, John Brown, Claudio William Veloso, Michel Briand, Francisco Gonzalez, Angela Curran, Gene Fendt, Monte Ransome Johnson, Eric Csapo, John Bussanich, and Antonio Attisani. Especially given the slurs that were cast my way from the beginning by others and the anger directed at me for challenging such an ingrained tenet as catharsis being the goal of tragedy in general—as opposed to being the goal of comedy or of one of the four sub-species of tragedy that the Northern Greek describes briefly in Chapter 18—I will always appreciate the moral, psychological, and philosophical support these scholars have offered.

I even appreciate, and must acknowledge, the rigorous

Introduction

attempt by Stephen Halliwell (*Between Ecstasy and Truth*, 2011) to refute my "Purging the *Poetics*" (*Oxford Studies in Ancient Philosophy*, 2003), which itself was the first publication to argue for the inauthenticity of catharsis, pity and fear in Chapter 6 (but the legitimacy of pity and fear in Chapters 13 & 14). Halliwell presents superb arguments based on the texts, which, however, I believe my subsequent work (notably *Aristotle on Dramatic Musical Composition*, 2nd ed., 2018, Chapter 6) completely and systematically refutes. Veloso and a world-renowned French ancient Greek specialist Marwan Rashed have also devastatingly replied to Halliwell. Nevertheless, rather than spitting out *ad hominem* arguments, Halliwell proceeds in the manner that any serious philosopher and lover of Aristotle should follow, and the British scholar's work, even if it does not succeed, helps us all better understand the subtleties of the Stagirite's thought.

Delia Cadman created the cover art, representing the singing rhapsode wearing a gold crown because of Plato's description of the famous rhapsode Ion in the dialogue of the same name (see, for example, Stephanus passages 535c, 535d, and 541c).

Gregory L. Scott
New York City, 2020

Aristotle DRAMATICS

Updates

For "digital extensions" to this book,
including any Errata or Updates,
please see:

www.epspress.com/Dramatics/Updates.html

Aristotle

DRAMATICS

Introduction

Aristotle DRAMATICS

Introduction

The Title and Nature of the Book

The book that has been known as the *Poetics* or *On the Art of Poetry*, based on the first two words of the manuscript copies, *peri poiētikēs*, has not one poem. Because there was no commentary on the treatise in antiquity or Byzantine times, it was given this title by the Arabic scholars who first wrote about it in detail starting in the 10th century, but who were working apparently with an Arabic translation of a Syriac translation of a presumed copy of the Greek manuscript made about 700 CE, a "mere" 1000 years after Aristotle's death.

However, the Arabic scholars (notably Avicenna and Averroes) had no first-hand understanding of theatrical drama, which was not unusual because even Western Europeans at that time had no direct knowledge of performances like tragedy and comedy after the time of Justinian, the repressive Christian emperor who forbade all such representations around 528 CE and who destroyed many of the relevant sources, including texts, from ancient Greece. It would not be until the late 1400's that scholars from Italy began working directly from the rediscovered remaining Greek manuscripts, trying to establish what the words meant, but even they continued the tradition set by the Arabs. Long after the rediscoveries, Averroes's commentary that interpreted Aristotle's dramatic principles as "ethical rhetoric" flourished, even with the Christian scholars. In part this was because Jewish, Christian and Muslim scholars intermingled and learned from each other in Toledo, Spain, an acclaimed center of learning for the age.

As glossed over because of the literary bias by the Arabic scholars and those coming after them, the paradigm, tragedy, which is examined in most of the chapters, has music in its definition and in the immediate explanation in Chapter 6, among other passages throughout the work. Thus, tragedy as analyzed in the treatise cannot be a form of poetry in our sense, notwithstanding that tragedy's definition involves verse as one of six necessary elements for Aristotle, because poetry for us means unadorned language in meter. Otherwise, if combined with music, it is song.

Commentators almost to a person have shockingly contended or implied that Aristotle not only ignores his multiple statements that all tragedies have six necessary elements but claims at the end of Chapter 6 that music and performance are merely optional or "imagined," with the language being the only element absolutely required. However, the Greek text clearly states that spectacle (*opsis*) is a *necessary* element, even if Aristotle adds that it "has *least* to do with the art of *dramatic musical composition*."

The latter statement, though, does not entail that spectacle is unnecessary for tragedy. Avicenna and Averroes had an excuse for making "spectacle" (like the sets and costumes) optional because they had no under-

Introduction

standing of performed ancient drama and completely misconstrued the term *opsis*. Commentators from the 1500's onwards knowing ancient Greek and having a basic understanding of performed drama from the 5th century BCE onwards have no excuse, and the time is long past to call out any of them who continue to write about tragedy in the *Dramatics* as if it were mere literature. This is a rank distortion, to say the very least, and one hardly need be a sublime philologist to understand the difference between "least" and "none" or between "least necessary" and "unnecessary."

These are just a few of the many reasons given in my *Aristotle on Dramatic Musical Composition: The Real Role of Literature, Catharsis, Music and Dance in the POETICS* (hereafter *ADMC*)[1] for entitling the Northern Greek's book instead *On the Art of Dramatic Musical Composition* or, for brevity, *The Dramatics*.

---

1   Gregory L. Scott, *Aristotle on Dramatic Musical Composition: The Real Role of Literature, Catharsis, Music and Dance in the POETICS*, New York: ExistencePS Press, 2nd ed., 2018 (originally published 2016).

The Core Greek Terms

Classicists immediately ask: "What about the first two words *peri poiētikēs*? Don't they mean, strictly speaking, 'on (the art of) poetry' or for short 'the poetics'?"

Poiētikēs and its more basic cognate *poiēsis* fundamentally meant "making," "doing" or "composing" until the time of Plato. Around 415 BCE, when the Athenian was a youngster, the sophist Gorgias gave *poiēsis* a special meaning, which later generations took on: "language in meter," that is, verse or poetry.

Yet Plato gives the proper sense in this context for the Greeks, at least until that moment in history, via his character Diotima, who has been primarily known for teaching Socrates the meaning of love in the dialogue *The Symposium*. She says that the meaning of *poiēsis* is broadly "making" but that more properly it is used *only* as "composition in 'music' and verse," whatever 'music' (*mousikē*) means in this context, and there are three choices: "arts of the Muses," "music," or "music-dance." Diotima's explanation has been available in manuscripts since even before the Renaissance but has been completely and inexplicably ignored in this context, even by the renowned modern female scholars of Plato and Aristotle.

Why all specialists have ignored Diotima concerning the aesthetics of Plato and Aristotle, when she is one of the few women in ancient times or at least one of the

Introduction

two female characters in the Platonic dialogues to be acclaimed, is utterly beyond me, and I have yet to hear a classicist explain the lack of attention. Suffice it to say here that I introduced her explanation in 1999 in "The *Poetics* of Performance,"[2] without naming her but while providing her explanation with the Stephanus number 205c (the numbering that allows any reader of Plato to find the exact passage).

Starting in 2016, I began publishing her importance, with her name, along with more details on the significance of her explanation. By grasping that Aristotle actually follows not the Gorgian-English meaning of *poiēsis* but the Diotiman "narrow" meaning (as "'music' and verse") and by understanding other Platonic and Aristotelian texts that prove the ambiguous *mousikē* means "music-dance" *in this context* and that Aristotle adds a fourth condition, plot, to make *poiēsis* a technical term in the Lyceum, we are able to resolve easily a number of heretofore unresolvable dilemmas, like why the Northern Greek did not cover *any* of the many genres of verse *per se* in a treatise always called until now *The Poetics* or *On the Art of Poetry*.

Aristotle only cares about tragedy, comedy and epic in the work because these are the forms of creation

---

2 Gregory L. Scott, "The *Poetics* of Performance: The Necessity of Performance, Spectacle, Music, and Dance in Aristotelian Tragedy," in *Performance and Authenticity in the Arts (Cambridge Series on Philosophy and the Arts)*, eds. Salim Kemal and Ivan Gaskell (Cambridge: Cambridge University Press, 1999) 15-48.

that had music, verse and dance, with, as suggested, gestures by the epic rhapsodes counting as dance or "ordered body movement" for the Greeks, as set forth by Plato at *Laws* II 665a. Better yet, they are the forms that have those three so-called "means of mimesis" (as given in *Dramatics* Chapter 1) *and that have plot*, which itself is stressed from the very first sentence. The only major mystery in this regard, then, is why satyr play, the final type of drama for the Greeks with the three means of mimesis and plot, is not covered in the extant treatise, but one option is that it was examined in the lost manuscript on comedy, the topic that originally finished our extant treatise.

Other Greek terms have been wrongly translated for generations. For instance, *rhuthmos* has been given its transliterated meaning "rhythm," which allows it to be applicable to language or literary theory but which then triggers irresolvable dilemmas, especially in Chapters 1, 4 and 6. By recognizing that the Greek words, like English words, are equivocal, with rich meanings, and by realizing that Aristotle follows *Laws* II 665a and always uses *rhuthmos* as "ordered body composition" or dance while discussing the orchestral arts (contrary to its meaning in the *Rhetoric*, which is relevant to a single speaker in law or government), many other perennial dilemmas simply dissolve. It becomes obvious, then, that the Northern Greek speaks about the cultural practices of his day but with a philosophical motivation, a delightful implication for one of the greatest empiricists of all time.

Introduction

To understand equivocity more, and to see that the meanings of words are not only dependent on the exact context but sometimes just on the combination of a direct object in a sentence, take the utterance: "Nick will play Creon in the play *Antigone* tonight, but I can't see the performance because I have to play my tennis match, nor can his wife Barbara because she will play the violin in her concert." No English speaker has a problem grasping that the verb "play" has three variant meanings in one and the same (complex) sentence, all determined by the direct object.

The Greeks were no different and sometimes the trick in ancient exegesis is not to try to find some magical univocal meaning of a word but to determine the best option among the various possible connotations the term could have in ancient Greece or in an ancient text, because sometimes authors like Aristotle give a word a technical meaning that is not found in common parlance. (I defy any reader to provide a single meaning of "play" that will convey the meanings in the complex sentence just given.)

Another classic example of equivocity regarding the *Dramatics* pertains to the core term *mimēsis*. The origin of our "mimetic," *mimēsis* can mean "imitation," "impersonation," "representation," "expression," or "copy." Commentators for centuries have tried to establish a univocal meaning that Aristotle uses, which is absurd. "Imitation" and "representation" are probably the most common translations and insofar as painting is spoken of by Aristotle, the translations are apt (although the Northern Greek recognizes somewhat favorably painting that was neither). Purely tonal or "formal" music, however, often does not "imitate" or "represent" anything unless it is another (sequence of) sounds. "Express" is typically the better translation in that setting, where music expresses (and not imitates) emotions or moods. If Martha is engaged in *mimēsis* of another person or animal (the origin of *mimēsis* in the 5th century BCE), it might be allowable to say "imitate," but "impersonate" is often more accurate.

Just as with "play," we would best recognize the richness of this word, and other Greek words, and in some passages translate a word one way for Aristotle and in other passages, even on the same page, translate it differently. Otherwise, we would have the same situation as a culture with a different language 2000 years from now, discovering the complex sentence with "play," after catastrophes had destroyed most English books, and forcing "play" to have one meaning while trying to make sense of the sentence in the new language.

Seven important, traditionally misunderstood core terms are, in alphabetical order:
1. *harmonia*: The goddess of Harmony; a fitting together (as planks in a ship); music; song (e.g. *Laws* II 665a). It is too often badly translated as "(musical) harmony" in this setting, when no musical harmony in our sense of the word

existed in ancient Greek music, in the sense of chords and chordal harmonies. Music was generally just single melodic lines, especially for Plato, who did not like the developments in so-called New Music of the 5th and 4th centuries BCE. Aristotle is a little more open-minded given, e.g., *Politics* VIII 7, but he still follows Plato in many ways and he generally uses *harmonia* in the *Dramatics* as music.

2. *lexis*: Speech, language, diction, and style. In the *Dramatics,* it typically means speech or language although on an occasion or two diction might be apt. In Chapters 19-20 it actually is very broad and subsumes *logos*, which I do not consider one of the core misunderstood terms, because all classicists know it has about two pages of different meanings in the standard Greek lexicons, including speech, language, prose (in contrast to *metron*, that is, verse), ratio, and proportion.

3. *melos/melopoiia*: "*-poiia*" is just a form of *poiēsis*, "making," so the second word is simply "the making of the *melos*." Once one determines what *melos* is, one knows what *melopoiia* conveys. *Melos* means primarily "limb" (like arm or leg) but is usually translated in the *Dramatics* as "melody." But this is too narrow usually, especially in a work that is not a technical musical treatise. Rather the other meanings, like "music" or the too rarely recognized "music-dance" (obviously associ-

ated with the moving limbs of the chorus that was singing and dancing), are often more suitable. In Chapter 6 only "music-dance" solves a perennial dilemma.

4. *metron*: "meter" as in music or in poetry. Thus, by extension or by synecdoche (referring to a whole by its part), it often means verse in contrast to prose.

5. *mousikē* has been noted already. It can mean "art of the Muses," or "music" or be synonymous with *melos* as "music-dance." We will see that the Stagirite uses it in this last sense in Chapter 26 (and my previous work has shown that he uses it exactly as music-dance in *Politics* VIII 7), following Plato's similar usage at times in *Laws* II.

6. *poiēsis* has already been noted. It has been traditionally always taken in the Gorgian sense (whether or not translators knew that Gorgias was responsible for its first use as "poetry" in the *Encomium to Helen* around 415 BCE). I employ the Diotiman "narrow" meaning of music, dance and verse, but show in *ADMC* that Aristotle restricts it further by adding plot as a fourth necessary and sufficient condition. To emphasize, *poiēsis* is thus a technical term in the book for Aristotle and for his school, sometimes called the Lyceum and sometimes the Peripatos.[3]

---

[3] The members of Aristotle's circle became known as Peripatetics, from the Greek meaning "turn around,"

7. *tragōidia*: typically translated as "tragedy," the usual (but not unanimous) account is that it came from "goat-song," perhaps because a goat was awarded as a prize to the winner of a dramatic competition (or burnt as an offering). Rather, whatever the origin, in the *Dramatics* it must mean most of the time "serious drama" for the upcoming reasons given in Chapters 13 and 14 and because three times the Northern Greek says that this type of play can go from fortune to misfortune *or vice-versa.*

In short, the *Dramatics* is not about literature *per se*, notwithstanding that verse is indeed *one* important element of drama, but about the kind of musical theater that is akin to our Broadway musicals or to our opera. However, the latter is generally categorized under music, and for Aristotle we will see that plot and language are more important than music, all of which means that Broadway musicals would be the more accurate modern parallel of ancient Greek tragedy and comedy. By understanding all of this a host of other problems are finally resolved and we arrive at a very accurate picture of what the Northern Greek was trying to accomplish in his book.

---

because they sometimes held advanced seminars in a garden of the establishment, while walking. Hence, when they came to a wall, they had to turn around to continue walking and conversing.

Single Treatise or Amalgamation?

"His book" (singular) is actually a misrepresentation. As one of the greatest German specialists of Aristotle and of ancient Greek philosophy, Eduard Zeller, once recognized, it has interpolations and inversions, with some chapters out of place. However, I have argued that Zeller misjudged which chapters were interpolated and inverted. For instance, for reasons already published, some of which are repeated below, Chapter 12 on the chorus is legitimate but whether it would fit in between other chapters on plot (11 and 13) is very questionable. Why would Aristotle break up the discussion of plot, which is explicitly his most important condition in the definition of tragedy and which he analyzes for multiple chapters right after the explanation of the definition?

The original *Dramatics* seems to have been significantly less in some ways than the extant text and more in others. The commonly recognized way in which the original was more pertains to the lost examination of comedy, which Aristotle promises at the beginning of Chapter 6. One line of manuscripts (of the four branches that have come down to us via different copyists and geographical regions in Europe, Africa and the Middle East) has words indicating that comedy was being treated after our final chapter (Chapter 26). However, seemingly because this portion was on a

Introduction

different papyrus, it is lost.[4]

Some previously unrecognized ways in which the original treatise is less than what we have, I have argued previously, is that Chapters 17 and 18 were interpolated, because Aristotle seems to refer to (the content of) Chapter 17 at the end of Chapter 15 as his "published work." In addition, Chapter 18 has four subspecies of tragedy that are never discussed as such anywhere else in the book and the discussion involves points that are inconsistent with the other chapters.

Another heretofore unrecognized way in which the extant treatise is less is that some parts of the *Rhetoric* dealing with metaphor may actually have been in the original *Dramatics*. That is, most of the material on language, dealing inappropriately with mere grammar and the like, were interpolated when Aristotle's library, which, according to tradition, had been buried in a trench to hide it from the book-robbing kings of Pergamum, was sold to the entrepeneur Apellicon, redone too hastily and re-sold for profit in Athens (and then in Rome). Somebody, probably under the direction of Apellicon, patched together the various, mixed up sections of papyri in a way that made sense to them but which, I believe, are impossible as part of a single organic whole that some scholars, despite Zeller,

---

4 The lost manuscript is the subject of the well-known film and thriller, *The Name of the Rose* (1986), with Sean Connery, based on the novel by the renowned Italian literary critic and semiotician Umberto Eco.

think we now have.⁵ This is more understandable when one realizes that Greek papyri had no titles on them, as of course modern books do. Nor did they have page numbers because each papyrus, be it equivalent to our page or chapter, was a continuous sheet that was rolled and unrolled. Nor did they have Tables of Contents or Bibliographies or Indices. They were stand-alone creatures, ranging, as it were, from the size of cats (if not ants, were we to consider fragments) to elephants.

The blatant inconsistencies between various chapters, even if for the sake of argument they are considered a unit, are discussed in detail in my *A Primer on Aristotle's DRAMATICS*.⁶ This book presents the basics of the very large *ADMC* and is intended for use with any traditional translation from a good publishing house. If one wishes to see how readers and commentators for generations understood the treatise, in about one-quarter the length of *ADMC,* this *Primer* gives the new approach alongside the old (but, again, presupposes that the reader is using the Greek text

---

5 To my knowledge, the most ardent defender of the view that the *Dramatics* is an organic whole, who best describes many of the problems and inconsistencies in the treatise, is Stephen Halliwell (*Aristotle's Poetics*, Chapel Hill and London: The University of North Carolina Press, 1986, especially pp. 31-37). Nevertheless, Halliwell misses a number of problems, takes the core Greek "musical" terms (and *poiēsis*) in the wrong, traditional way, and in my view is too forgiving of the tensions raised by the inconsistencies.

6 Gregory L. Scott, *A Primer on Aristotle's DRAMATICS (also known as the POETICS)*, New York: ExistencePS Press, 2019.

Introduction

itself or a good, traditional translation).

Whether read as before, with the 26 chapters in sequence as an organic whole, or not, there are seven badly misunderstood core terms and 10 mangled chapters. My translation here gives occasional footnotes to highlight a few of the corrections of the old view, but for a rigorous explanation of those differences, again, see *A Primer*.

One dilemma for me was whether to strip out the interpolated chapters and add them as an Appendix entitled "Miscellaneous Additional Texts of Aristotle on the Same Subject" or to keep the traditional chapters and note the oddities. Each approach has advantages and disadvantages. I chose the latter approach with the exception of breaking Chapter 14 into two, 14A and 14B, as I explain later.

Catharsis

Another problem with understanding the Stagirite's motivations and overall theory in the treatise stems from the infamous catharsis-clause in the definition of tragedy in Chapter 6: "tragedy is a serious representation ... *through pity and fear accomplishing the catharsis of such emotions.*" Ever since the first commentary by Avicenna, no one has been able to understand the word *katharsis* in this chapter *and* to translate it in a way that is consistent not only with ancient Greek usage, as "purification," "purgation" or "clarification," but with the rest of Aristotle's well understood doctrines.

In addition, pity and fear are sometimes good emotions for him and to purge them would be inappropriate. Purifying pity so that we have pure pity is shocking as a goal and would exclude any mixture with fear; likewise pure fear would rule out any pity, as Aristotle explicitly says in the *Rhetoric*. Clarifying what the emotions are is for teachers, not dramatists whose goal, given many statements in the treatise, is to give a (proper) pleasure or enjoyment.

Also, as mentioned, the Northern Greek says three times in the *Dramatics* that *tragōidia* can have protagonists going from fortune to misfortune or vice-versa. If all of this were not enough, the best type of *tragōidia* in Chapter 14 is explicitly the one that ends happily, like *Cresphontes* or *Iphigenia* (presum-

Introduction

ably *in Tauris* because the variant *Iphigenia in Aulis* ends unhappily)! Thus "tragedy" is a very misleading translation in modern English for *tragōidia* and the better rendering is "serious drama." This rendering was obscured in part because, until M.D. Petruševski in 1947, readers always thought that the catharsis-clause was completely legitimate.

However, it is hard to get away from "tragedy" and although I will continue to use it in a technical sense from this point onwards without the quotation marks, I emphasize the previous caveats. Tragedy is that which is defined in Chapter 6 *minus the (wrongly interpolated) catharsis-clause.*

Without the implication of a necessarily bad ending and for other reasons pertaining to Aristotle's theory of definition, catharsis, pity and fear can be seen to be inauthentic. Indeed, Aristotle says in Chapter 13 that serious plays with the virtuous protagonist (*epieikēs*) going from fortune to misfortune *has no pity nor fear*, because such a plot is shocking or disgusting (*miaron*). If there is no pity and fear, *a fortiori* there can be no catharsis *of* pity and fear. What has thrown scholars for generations is that in the same chapter Aristotle accepts Oedipus to be the finest type of tragedy *with pity and fear*.

As I explain in detail in *Aristotle's Favorite Tragedy: Oedipus or Cresphontes?*,[7] the way to resolve the

---

7   Gregory L. Scott, *Aristotle's Favorite Tragedy: Oedipus*

contradiction of the best types of tragedy between Chapters 13 and 14 is to consider the ranking of Chapter 14 to be of tragedy *in general* and the ranking of Chapter 13 to be of a *particular subtype* of tragedy, one which ends badly and which *should* have pity and fear. As we see in Chapter 18, Aristotle outlines four subtypes of tragedy but there is no discussion of them as such in the rest of the book, and two subtypes—tragedy of character and tragedy of suffering—are completely missing, all of which helps prove Zeller's point that the extant book is corrupt and incomplete. Just because pity and fear are relevant to one subtype in no way means the two emotions are relevant to all subtypes, especially given the Stagirite's explicit statements about the plot with a virtuous person going to misfortune not involving them.

In *ADMC* I give the rigorous arguments and evidence for why Aristotle could not have written himself *katharsis* in the definition of tragedy,[8] and I go beyond Petruševski to show why pity and fear were also badly interpolated by a later editor, one reason

---

or *Cresphontes?*, New York: ExistencePS Press, 2nd edition 2018 (orig. publ. 2016).

8   The arguments were first published in "Purging the *Poetics*," *Oxford Studies in Ancient Philosophy*, Vol. 25 (Winter 2003) 233-264. The article is reproduced as Chapter 5 in *ADMC* and I correct one mistake there regarding pity and fear occurring (simply) in the best plots for Aristotle, when I should have said in 2003 (as I explain in *ADMC*) that the emotions are relevant to the best plots *that end badly,* as primarily discussed in Chapter 13 (and 14A).

Introduction

being just given, namely, the statements in Chapter 13. In this translation, then, I athetize that whole catharsis-clause, that is, I bracket it as inauthentic (or, what amounts to the same, I cross it out). Nevertheless, I keep the crossed-out words, so that readers will understand where they occurred in case they run across any of the thousands of discussions of the topic occurring over 500 years.

As a result, the treatise becomes not only more consistent internally but externally, especially concerning *Politics* VIII 3-7, where *enjoyment* is the best end of the "musical arts." Historically, many dramatists, Racine and Brecht being two of the most famous, have rejected Aristotle in part because they found it implausible that catharsis is the goal of tragedy. They have found the goal of catharsis to be unempirical, a wounding criticism to one of the greatest empiricists in the history of philosophy, but a criticism that we see is unwarranted once we see that the catharsis-clause is inauthentic. A proper pleasure is indeed a much more sensible goal for the vast range of serious dramatic plays, not only around the 4th century BCE, but onwards to this day.

Needless to say, this rejection of the legitimacy of catharsis will have grave implications for the historical cultural practices, such as dramatic or literary theory, that have been shaped by Aristotle's view over the centuries. The influence has been felt even in psychology because the concept was central to the younger Freud, who married the niece of Jacob Bernays. Bernays was probably the most influential commentator in the 19th century of the (*Dramatics aka*) *Poetics* and argued against the famous view of Gotthold Lessing (1729-1781) that catharsis in Chapter 6 meant (a moral) purification, claiming that the term instead for Aristotle had the medical sense of "purgation."

My works and those of a number of internationally recognized scholars who are following me in various ways, help show that catharsis was primarily, if not wholly, relevant to *comedy* for the Northern Greek (which even famous Aristotelian specialists like W.D. Ross accepted to a certain extent in the early 1900's). Given the promise in *Politics* VIII 7 of an *explanation* of catharsis in a *peri poiētikēs,* the explanation was almost surely presented in the lost book on comedy (unless there was another, lost treatise with the same title). This is because, as the reader will soon quickly discover firsthand, there is absolutely no explanation in the extant work, all of which belies the attempts over centuries to justify catharsis in *tragedy* based on the promise in VIII 7.

Introduction

Why not an Original Translation?

One does not destroy a beautiful Victorian mansion (or indeed any noteworthy home) and rebuild from scratch just because the windows are badly fogged, some of the doors are sticking, the roof leaks in a few spots, and one corner of a porch is rotting. Rather, assuming the foundation and structure are sound, one repairs it for perhaps $1/100^{th}$ of the cost and effort.

Likewise, why start a translation of a famous Greek text from scratch when there are dozens of good ones and some superb ones already in English (and hundreds if not thousands more in other languages over many centuries)? I need only replace the renderings of about seven core Greek terms and the ten significantly affected chapters that were misunderstood for generations, and tweak some of the other passages. Like the architectural repair, the emendation seems much more prudent, and hence the current approach.[9] I take, therefore, one of the most respected and influential translations of the last 100 years, Ingram Bywater's from 1920, which is included, and therefore vetted, by Jonathan Barnes for *The Complete Works of Aristotle: The Revised Oxford Translation*, Vol. 2, 1984, and I change only the badly interpreted Greek.

A further word of caution: Barnes uses the standard Greek text of his day, of Rudolf Kassell from 1965, to

---

[9] I am grateful to Monte Ransome Johnson, who (easily) persuaded me to take this route.

make decisions about which Greek words should be athetized or not, given the discrepancies in the four branches of manuscripts that have survived, with about 31 total copies throughout the Western world. Barnes revises Bywater's translation accordingly, with, for instance, *kai melos* in Chapter 6 (1449b29[10]) being completely omitted, in large part if not wholly because no one had been able to make sense in that sentence of the word *melos* given traditional translations (see the section above on *melos*); *kai* simply means "and" or "that is." Yet, as we shall see, one cannot make full, correct sense of Chapter 6 without truly understanding *melos* and its synonym *melopoiia* ("the making of the *melos*") there. Leonardo Tarán and Dimitri Gutas supersede Kassell's Greek with *Aristotle Poetics: Editio Maior* in 2012, and I rely on it.[11]

As praiseworthy as Tarán and Gutas's work is and as indispensable as it will be for all serious specialists of the *Dramatics*, notably from the paleographical perspective (which shows, for example, that *kai melos* in Chapter 6 should *not* be excised), one must be very

---

10 "1449b29" is the Bekker number, which, similar to the Stephanus number for Plato, allows one to find the exact line in a manuscript by Aristotle (or in translations for scholarly use). The manuscripts have two columns "a" and "b," so for the just-cited line, 1449 is the page number, "b" is the second column, and 29 is the line.

11 Leonardo Tarán and Dimitri Gutas, *Aristotle Poetics: Editio Maior of the Greek Text with Historical Introduction and Philological Commentaries* (Brill: Leiden and Boston, 2012).

Introduction

careful with their philology concerning the core Greek words noted above. They do not even recognize, for example, the applicability of Diotima's explanation of *poiēsis* and continue with the wrong tradition of merely assuming the Gorgian meaning. Perhaps I should say "Tarán" rather than "they," because he is primarily or solely responsible for the Greek and Gutas for the Arabic, but it is hard to imagine that Gutas did not also proof the philological conclusions. At any rate, we must be even more careful of their philosophical interpretations, as covered in my *ADMC* and in other scholars' reviews or books.[12]

In brief, I avail myself of Tarán and Gutas's work

---

12 *ADMC* Vol. 1, pp. 12; 158; 205; 214; 217-8; 220; 221 footnote 348; and 229-30; Vol. 2, pp. 377; 380 footnote 550; 386; 397 footnote 592; 408-9 footnote 612; 422; 445-6; 448 footnote 675; 452-3; 524; 527-8; 559 footnote 843; and 592 footnote 938.

Additional commentary is provided in my *A Primer to Aristotle's DRAMATICS,* pp. 28-30; 40-1; 87-8; 94; 97-100; 113; 121-2 footnote 104; 142; 158-9 footnote 133; 160; 173-4; 249; 256; 269 footnote 209; 266 footnote 213; 269-71; 274 footnote 221; 281-84; 287; 290; 294; and 297-8.

See also Richard Janko, book review of Tarán and Gutas, in Book Reviews, *Classical Philology* 108 (2013) 252–7, which is also at:
http://www-personal.umich.edu/~rjanko/review%20Gutas%20&%20Tar%E1n.pdf

Finally, suffice it to say here that other disputes, and other disputes of even the paleography, are presented by Claudio William Veloso in *Pourquoi la Poétique d'Aristote? DIAGOGÈ*, with a Preface by Marwan Rashed (Paris: Vrin, 2018): pp. 70-1; 151; 184; 244; 255-7; 271; 282; 298; 303; 335-40; 348; 374; and 377.

primarily to resolve issues of the core Greek terms and their applicability. Subtle matters of a letter or a minor word or extremely fine points of Greek grammar that are shown by their apparatus to involve conflicts in the different manuscripts are usually left aside. I almost invariably accept their choices in those regards and sincerely applaud them for their rigor in terms of the associated paleography, but those issues will have absolutely bearing on the crucial theses of this translation.

If readers wish to compare the original translation by Bywater to mine they can easily find an inexpensive paperback online or they can use the free version at the Project Gutenberg:

www.gutenberg.org/ebooks/6763

Another commendable translation, with many extremely illuminating footnotes of various aspects of Greek drama and related issues, that is freely available is the one by W.H. Fyfe,[13] also available at the Perseus Project:

www.perseus.tufts.edu/hopper/text?doc=Perseus:text:1999.01.0056

Because Fyfe's version has both English and Greek,

---

13   *Aristotle in 23 Volumes*, Vol. 23, translated by W.H. Fyfe (Cambridge, MA, Harvard University Press; London, William Heinemann Ltd., 1932).

with the Bekker numbers for each language, I refer any reader wishing to determine precise line numbers to it (or to the edition by Tarán and Gutas, which, again, though, has no translation). However, Fyfe, like Bywater, unsurprisingly (if sadly) takes the core Greek terms in the traditional, mistaken way.

Lastly, another book worth using as a resource is Richard Janko's *Aristotle: Poetics, with the Tractatus Coisilianus, Reconstruction of Poetics II, and the Fragments of the On Poets*.[14] Even though Janko, like everyone else, mostly just assumes the traditional but mistaken interpretations of the core Greek terms and, ignoring Aristotle's theory of definition, also assumes the legitimacy of catharsis in the definition of tragedy, he nevertheless provides valuable insights into the obscure dramatists and ancient references. He adds fragments of related texts, one of which *On Poets*, is also badly titled given the emphasis on music and drama shown in the fragments that Janko himself translates. Given how the Northern Greek follows Plato-Diotima, the title should be *On Dramatic Musical Composers* or perhaps for short *On Musical Composers* or *On Composers*.

In my Commentary (Introduction, footnotes and bracketed insertions within the translation), as the

---

14 Richard Janko, *Aristotle: Poetics, with the Tractatus Coisilianus, Reconstruction of Poetics II, and the Fragments of the On Poets* (Indianapolis: Hackett Publishing Company, 1987).

reader has already begun to notice, I use American punctuation. Out of respect for Bywater's original and for his heritage, and in part to emphasize the difference in authors, I keep the British punctuation for the translation *per se*.

Introduction

Summary and Principles

This translation abides by at least these principles:

1. Aristotle follows Plato and Diotima on *poiēsis* being "music-dance and verse" rather than the sophist Gorgias's "poetry" (that is, language and meter). However, the Stagirite restricts the term further by adding "plot" (*muthos*) to complete the four necessary and sufficient conditions for something to be within scope. *Muthos* (as explained in Chapter 6) is *not* "the structure of the actions *in words*" but simply the "structure of the actions" or, as Bywater translates, "the combination of the incidents." In this sense, plot would be easily recognized by Aristotle not only in a story-ballet (as suggested in Chapters 1 and 4) but in our silent films that have no words.

2. Related to this is the lack of "poet" and "poetry" in the translation, especially when pertaining to figures like Homer. Noburo Notomi, in an exemplary piece of modern scholarship, demonstrates that Homer and the other earlier "creators" were called "singers" and the like, *not* "poets."[15]

---

15 As Notomi writes:
> the general term of 'making' (*poiēsis*) was relatively new in the time of Plato, which had just come to be used for the specific activity of poetry... The word contains a wider sense of making of *logos*, so that it sometimes includes *prose-writing*... What *we* call 'poetry' had a long history already at the time of Plato; the two poets, Homer and Hesiod,

3. *Rhuthmos kai harmonia* always means "dance and music" rather than "rhythm and harmony" for Aristotle in the *Dramatics* (and in *Politics* VIII and likewise for Plato in *Laws* II, especially at 665a, except for one demonstrable change of meaning at 672 that for once is our "rhythm").

4. *Mousikē* means "music-dance" at times for Plato and for Aristotle (as in *Dramatics* 26 and in *Politics* VIII 7) and *melos* at times is synonymous, as in *Dramatics* 6.

5. Many terms, like *mimēsis*, are equivocal, and we

---

were respected and of great authority in Greek civilization. *However, 'poiēsis' and its cognate Greek words came to mean 'poetry' etc. relatively late in the history.* Homer and Hesiod *never* described their activity and products in terms of 'poetry' (*poiēsis*), 'making poems' (*poiein*), 'poem' (*poiēma*), 'poet' (*poiētēs*), and 'poetic' (*poiētikos*). Judging from the extant literature, it was probably in the mid or late fifth century BCE that these words came into use. *Before the term 'poetry' was introduced in the generic sense, the performer and performance had been called 'singer' (aoidos) and 'singing', or 'song' (aoidē)...*

Noburu Notomi, "Image-Making in *Republic* X and the *Sophist*," in *Plato and the Poets*, ed. by P. Destrée and F. Herrmann (Leiden & Boston: Brill, 2011) 300-4; my italics.

Ignoring the chronology, I should add that many renowned classicists over the last 25 years have confirmed Notomi's view: Pindar, Sappho and others make *songs*, not poems. In effect, for generations, music has been unduly stripped out of the early artistic culture of ancient Greece, primarily because it had no notation and only the words survived.

Introduction

need to determine the precise sense in any given passage to grasp best the Northern Greek's arguments.

6. *Tragōidia* for both Plato and Aristotle is not "tragedy" in our sense because, e.g., Aristotle says three times in the *Dramatics* that the play can show protagonists going from *misfortune to fortune*. Rather something like "serious drama" is a better translation. Moreover, the best serious dramas in Chapter 14 end happily and are ranked *above* the type like *Oedipus* that ends horribly.

7. Aristotle defines "tragedy" (used in a technical sense) in Chapter 6 to be a *necessarily* performed art with music, dance and spectacle, along with the language. It comes closest to our serious Broadway musical (rather than to our opera, because "music-dance" is ranked next to last in importance in the list of six necessary elements and opera would require that music be primary).

8. The Stagirite's book is about "musical" dramatic theory, not literature *per se*, and applying principles mechanically from one art form to another without sufficient justification not only ignores his adage from Chapter 25 that each art form has its own principles but distorts (and often weakens) his aesthetic principles.

9. Neither catharsis nor the couplet "pity and fear" is legitimate in the definition of serious drama in Chapter 6; rather the goal of the musical and

dramatic arts for Aristotle is (a proper) pleasure or "intellectual delight," as he explicitly says in *Dramatics* 23 in the definition of epic, where epic, *like tragedy*, gives its *proper pleasure*. (All of this is confirmed in general in *Politics* VIII for reasons given in previous publications by myself and others like Veloso.)

10. If catharsis was explained in the *Dramatics,* as suggested by *Politics* VIII 7, rather than in a completely lost treatise with the same name, the explanation had to have been in the lost section on comedy, and catharsis was primarily, if not exclusively, relevant to that art form rather than to *tragōidia* in Aristotle's mature work. The early dialogue *On (Dramatic) Musical Composers aka On Poets* might have been different, but this was because the Stagirite was greatly influenced as a student by Plato, who himself considers catharsis to be important in many areas of human life and philosophy.

11. The (*Dramatics aka*) *Poetics*, as Eduard Zeller once wrote, "shows many greater or smaller gaps, as also interpolation ... and inversions ... which sufficiently prove that we only possess Aristotle's work in a mutilated and hopelessly corrupt condition."[16]

---

16 From Costelloe, B.F.C. and J.H. Muirhead, *Aristotle and the Earlier Peripatetics: Being a Translation from Zeller's "Philosophy of the Greeks,"* in Two Volumes (New York: Russell & Russell, Inc., 1962), p. 103. In my *A Primer on*

Introduction

Aristotle's DRAMATICS, though, I show that the interpolations and inversions were sometimes not the ones that Zeller thought. I highlight a few of those issues, along with other matters, in the translation below, in footnotes or bracketed insertions in the body of the text.

Aristotle

DRAMATICS

DRAMATICS
Chapter 1

Our subject being dramatic 'musical' composition,[1] I propose to speak not only of the art in general but also of its species and their respective capacities; of the structure of plot required for a good composition; of the number and nature of the constituent parts of a work; and likewise of any other matters in the same line of inquiry. Let us follow the natural order and begin with the primary facts.

Epic composition and tragedy, as also comedy, dithyrambic composition, and most double-oboe playing and kithara playing, are all, viewed as a whole, modes of representation. But at the same time they differ from one another in three ways, either by a difference of kind in their *means*, or by differences in the *objects*, or in the *manner* of their representations.

Just as form and color are used as means by some, who (whether by art or constant practice) imitate and portray many things by their aid, and the voice is used by others; so also in the above-mentioned group

---

1   As discussed in the Commentary and for the extensive reasons given in *Aristotle on Dramatic Musical Composition* (*ADMC*), *peri poiētikēs*, like *poiēsis,* has a technical sense for Aristotle in the Lyceum, following but restricting Diotima: music, verse, dance *and plot*. The group of cognates do not mean (mere) "poetry." This is why I put "music" in quotations, because in the Greek sense it would really stand for "music-dance" here. With this caveat, and for simplicity, from now on I drop the quotation marks.

of arts, the means with them as a whole are dance, language, and music—used, however, *either singly or in certain combinations.*

A combination of dance and music by themselves is the means in double-oboe playing[2] and kithara playing, and in any other arts which have a similar function [in the choral sections in the theater], as, for example, pipe-playing.[3]

Dance alone, without music, is the means in the *corps de ballet's* impersonations; for even they, by the figured dances, may represent men's characters, as well as what they do and suffer.

There is further an art which represents by bare language, in prose or in verse, and if in verse, either in some one or in a plurality of metres. *This form of representation is to this day without a name.* We have no common name for a mime of Sophron or Xenarchus and a Socratic story; and we should still be without one even if the representation in the two instances were

---

[2] I use "double-oboe" for *aulos*, which had two pipes and which was a woodwind. Perhaps it should be called a "double clarinet." For hundreds of years, translators rendered it "flute," which is inaccurate. *Plagiaulos* is the term for the flute.

[3] "Pipe(-playing)" here is "panpipe" (*syrinx*), used by satyrs in satyr plays. Aristotle gives an example of the dancing double-oboe players at the beginning of Chapter 26 when he speaks of the bad ones whirling about when they represent a "discus" (presumably a "discus-throwing").

in trimeters or elegiacs or some other kind of verse—though it is the way with people to tack on 'composer' to the name of a metre, and talk of elegiac-composers and epic-composers, thinking that they call them composers not by reason of the representative nature of their work, but indiscriminately by reason of the metre they write in. Even if a theory of medicine or physical philosophy be put forth in a metrical form, it is usual to describe the maker in this way; Homer and Empedocles, however, have really nothing in common apart from their metre; so that, if the one is to be called a composer, the other should be termed a physicist rather than a composer.

We should be in the same position also, if the representation in these instances were in all the metres, like the *Centaur* (a rhapsody in a medley of all metres) of Chaeremon; and Chaeremon one has to recognize as a composer. So much, then, as to these arts.

There are, lastly, certain other arts, which combine *all the means* enumerated—dance, music, and verse—for instance, dithyrambic and nomic composition,[4]

---

4   The dithyramb is commonly understood but the nome rarely. E.F. Forster says: "of the only 'nome' of which the words have come down to us, the *Persae* of Timotheus ... resembles the meaningless libretto of an inferior opera and must have depended for its effect on the music and the mimetic powers of the performers" (*The Works of Aristotle*, Vol. II, *Problemata*, by E.F. Forster, under the editorship of W.D. Ross, Oxford: Clarendon Press, 1930; comment on 918b.)

tragedy and comedy; with this difference, however, that the three kinds of means are in some of them [dithyramb and nome] all employed together, and in others [like tragedy and comedy] brought in separately, one after the other. These elements of difference in the above arts I term the means of their representation.

Chapter 2

The objects the representor represents are actions, with agents who are necessarily either good men or bad—the diversities of human character being nearly always derivative from this primary distinction, since the line between virtue and vice is one dividing the whole of mankind.

It follows, therefore, that the agents represented must be either above our own level of goodness, or beneath it, or just such as we are in the same way as, with the painters, the personages of Polygnotus are better than we are, those of Pauson worse, and those of Dionysius just like ourselves.

It is clear that each of the above-mentioned arts will admit of these differences, and that it will become a separate art by representing objects with this point of difference. Even in dancing, double-oboe playing, and kithara playing such diversities are possible; and they are also possible in the nameless art that uses language, prose or verse [without music], as its means; Homer's personages, for instance, are better than we are; Cleophon's are on our own level; and those of Hegemon of Thasos, the first composer of parodies, and Nicochares, the author of the *Diliad*, are beneath it. The same is true of the dithyramb and the nome: the personages may be presented in them with the difference exemplified in the... of... and *Argas*, and in the *Cyclopses* of Timotheus and Philoxenus.[5]

This difference it is that distinguishes tragedy and comedy also; the one would make its personages worse, and the other better, than the men of the present day.

Chapter 3

A third difference in these arts is the manner in which each kind of object is represented. Given both the same means and the same kind of object for representation, one may either (1) speak at one moment in narrative and at another in an assumed character, as Homer does; or (2) one may remain the same throughout, without any such change; or (3) the impersonators may express the whole story dramatically, as though they were actually doing the things described.

As we said at the beginning, therefore, the differences in the representation of these arts come under three

---

5   The ellipsis "..." represents a gap in the manuscripts that has never been plausibly resolved.

heads, their means, their objects, and their manner.

So that as an impersonator Sophocles will be on one side akin to Homer, both portraying good men; and on another to Aristophanes, since both present their personages as acting and doing.

This in fact, according to some, is the reason for plays being termed dramas, because in a play the personages enact the story. Hence, too, both tragedy and comedy are claimed by the Dorians as their discoveries; comedy by the Megarians—by those in Greece as having arisen when Megara became a democracy, and by the Sicilian Megarians on the ground that the composer Epicharmus[6] was of their country, and a good deal earlier than Chionides and Magnes; even tragedy also is claimed by certain of the Peloponnesian Dorians. In support of this claim they point to the words 'comedy' and 'drama'. Their word for the outlying hamlets, they say, is *comae*, whereas Athenians call them *demes*—thus assuming that comedians got the name not from their *comoe* or revels, but from their strolling from hamlet to hamlet, lack of appreciation keeping them

---

6 Janko, in his Book Review of Tarán and Gutas, *op. cit.*, claims that "composer" (what he translates as "poet" for *poiētēs*) is redundant here and should be excised. But this need not be the case. As we will see in, e.g., Chapter 14, Aristotle often identifies a play by giving its maker (because sometimes plays by different dramatists had the same title), and identifying a person by giving his profession follows the same tactic. There could have been an Epicharmus who was not a dramatist. Hence I keep the word "composer."

out of the city. Their word also for 'to act', they say, is *dran*, whereas Athenians use *prattein*.

So much, then, as to the number and nature of the points of difference in the representation of these arts.

Chapter 4

It is clear that the general origin of dramatic musical composition was due to two causes, each of them part of human nature. Imitation is natural to man from childhood, one of his advantages over the lower animals being this, that he is the most imitative creature in the world and learns at first by imitation.

And it is also natural for all to delight in works of imitation. The truth of this second point is shown by experience: though the objects themselves may be painful to see, we delight to view the most realistic representations of them in art, the forms, for example, of the lowest animals and of dead bodies. The explanation is to be found in a further fact: to be learning something is the greatest of pleasures not only to the philosopher but also to the rest of mankind, however small their capacity for it; the reason of the delight in seeing the picture is that one is at the same time learning, [that is,] gathering the meaning of things, e.g. that the man there is so-and-so; for if one has not seen the thing before, one's pleasure will not be in the picture as a representation of it, but will be due to the execution or coloring or some similar cause.

Representation, then, being natural to us—as also music and dance (with metres being obviously species of ordered body movement)—it was through their original aptitude, and by a series of improvements for the most part gradual on their first efforts, that they created dramatic musical compositions out of their improvisations.

Dramatic musical composition, however, soon broke up into two kinds according to the differences of character in the individual composers; for the graver among them would represent noble actions, and those of noble personages; and the meaner sort the actions of the ignoble. The latter class produced invectives at first, just as others did hymns and panegyrics. We know of no such composition by any of the pre-Homeric creators, though there were probably many such composers among them; instances, however, may be found from Homer downwards, e.g. his *Margites*, and the similar works of others. In invective its natural fitness brought an iambic metre into use; hence our present term 'iambic', because it was the metre of their 'iambs' or invectives against one another. The result was that the old composers became some of them creators of heroic and others of iambic verse.

Homer's position, however, is peculiar: just as he was in the serious style the composer of composers, standing alone not only through goodness [of character]

DRAMATICS

but also through the dramatic quality of his impersonations, so too he was the first to outline for us the general forms of comedy by producing not a dramatic invective but a dramatic picture of the ridiculous; his *Margites* in fact stands in the same relation to our comedies as the *Iliad* and *Odyssey* to our tragedies. As soon, however, as tragedy and comedy appeared in the field, those naturally drawn to the one line of creation became makers of comedies instead of iambs, and those naturally drawn to the other, makers of tragedies instead of epics, because these new modes of art were grander and of more esteem than the old.

If it be asked whether tragedy is now all that it need be in its formative elements, to consider that, and decide it theoretically and in relation to the theatres, is a matter for another inquiry.[7]

It certainly began in improvisations—as did also comedy; the one originating with the 'starters' of the dithyramb,[8] the other with those of the phallic songs, which still survive as institutions in many of our cities.

---

7   Given that Aristotle has been discussing the origin of tragedy for two pages, it is puzzling that he returns to the origin as improvisation but now using dithyramb and phallic songs, not Homer, as the sources, without acknowledging the previous discussion. This may indicate yet again a combining of different Aristotelian texts by a later editor.

8   The "starters" were the primary leaders of the dithyramb, and as Aristotle has just suggested, they would improvise at least a prelude to the performance. Some believe they became the "first actors," like Thespis, whom Aristotle spoke of according to Themistius. More on Themistius shortly.

And its advance after that was little by little, through their improving on whatever they had before them at each stage. It was in fact only after a long series of changes that the movement of tragedy stopped on its attaining its natural form.

[Themistius (c. 317-390 CE) notes that Aristotle spoke of Thespis being the first actor; hence, our "thespian." (On some historical accounts, Thespis toured with wagons to enact the first dramas *per se*.) We have no other text in the whole Aristotelian corpus conveying this account and so the Stagirite's passage was lost. A reasonable assumption is that Thespis was mentioned here, before Aeschylus increases the number of actors to two in the next sentence.[9]]

The number of actors was first increased to two by Aeschylus, who curtailed the business of the chorus, and made the dialogue, or spoken portion, take the leading part in the play. A third actor and scenery were due to Sophocles. Tragedy acquired also its magnitude. Discarding short stories and a ludicrous diction, through its passing out of its satyric stage, it assumed, though only at a late point in its progress, a tone of dignity; and its metre changed then from trochaic to iambic. The reason for their original use of the trochaic tetrameter was that their creation was satyric and more connected with dancing than it now is. As soon, however, as a spoken part came in, nature herself found the appropriate metre. The iambic, we know, is the most speakable of metres, as is shown by the fact that we very often fall into it in conversation,

---

9   For details, see *ADMC* Vol. 1, pp. 159-60 footnote 242; 190-1 footnote 309; 289; Vol. 2 pp. 397-8.

whereas we rarely talk hexameters, and only when we depart from the speaking tone of voice. Another change was a plurality of episodes or acts.

As for the remaining matters, the superadded embellishments and the account of their introduction, these must be taken as said, as it would probably be a long piece of work to go through the details.

Chapter 5

As for comedy, it is (as has been observed) an impersonation of men worse than the average; worse, however, not as regards any and every sort of fault, but only as regards one particular kind, the ridiculous, which is a species of the ugly. The ridiculous may be defined as a mistake or deformity not productive of pain or harm to others; the mask, for instance, that excites laughter, is something ugly and distorted without causing pain.[10]

Though the successive changes in tragedy and their authors are not unknown, we cannot say the same of comedy; its early stages passed unnoticed, because it was not as yet taken up in a serious way. It was only at a late point in its progress that a chorus of comedians was officially granted by the archon; they used to be

---

10 Arguments and evidence for why Aristotle conceives of comedy also as dramatic musical composition to be performed in the theater have been given in my previous books. One point I always forgot to mention is that if comedy were merely literary, the point about the mask is irrelevant.

mere volunteers. It had also already certain definite forms at the time when the record of those termed 'comic composers' begins. Who it was who supplied it with masks, or prologues, or a plurality of actors and the like, has remained unknown. The invented plot, however, originated in Sicily, with Epicharmus and Phormis; of Athenian composers Crates was the first to renounce the comedy of invective and generalize the language and plots.

Epic, then, has been seen to agree with tragedy to this extent, that of being a representation of serious subjects in a grand kind of verse. It differs from it, however, (1) in that it is in one kind of verse and in narrative form; and (2) in its length—which is due to its action having no fixed limit of time, whereas tragedy endeavors to keep as far as possible within a single circuit of the sun, or something near that. This, I say, is another point of difference between them, though at first the practice in this respect was just the same in tragedies as in epic. They differ also (3) in their constituents, some being common to both and others peculiar to tragedy—hence a judge of good and bad in tragedy is a judge of that in epic also. All the parts of an epic are included in tragedy; but those of tragedy are not all found in epic.[11]

---

[11] As Chapters 23-26 make clearer, epic was sung by the rhapsode (and may have been partially "declaimed," similar to the vocal part of modern rap). It had, though, neither the choral singing and dancing, nor the spectacle, nor the actors helping enact the plot,—the parts "peculiar" to tragedy.

Chapter 6

Reserving representations in hexameter [= epic] and comedy for consideration hereafter, let us proceed now to the discussion of 'tragedy' [12]; before doing so, however, we must gather up the definition resulting from what has been said. A tragedy, then, is the impersonation of an action that is serious and also, as having magnitude, complete in itself; in language with pleasurable accessories, each kind brought in separately in the parts of the work; in a dramatic, not in a narrative form [~~with incidents arousing pity and fear, wherewith to accomplish its catharsis of such emotions~~].[13] Here by 'language with pleasurable accessories' I mean that with dance and music, namely, 'music-dance' [i.e., choral art] superadded; and by 'the kinds separately' I mean that some portions are worked out with verse only, and others in turn with

---

12   This term is in quotation marks because we will see that "serious play" is a better translation, given the rest of the book, in which Aristotle allows the drama to end happily and in which (in Chapter 14) the best "tragedies" *do* end happily. From this point on, the reader should consider "tragedy" to be a technical term, even if I drop the quotation marks, given how common the term is used historically.

13   As explained in the Commentary and rigorously in previous publications, this final clause was interpolated wrongly by a later editor; hence, there is no reason trying to translate it, especially because no one in 1000 years has successfully translated *katharsis* to the satisfaction of specialists. That is, no sense of the word understood in ancient Athens accords with the rest of Aristotle's well-accepted aesthetics, psychology, ethics and politics.

music-dance.

As they enact the expression, it follows that in the first place the spectacle (or stage-appearance of the actors) must be some part of the whole; and in the second choral art and speech, these two being the means of their representation. Here by 'speech' I mean merely this, the composition of the verses; and by (the making of the) 'choral art' what is too completely understood to require explanation. But further: the subject represented also is an action; and the action involves agents, who must necessarily have their distinctive qualities both of character and thought, since it is from these that we ascribe certain qualities to their actions. There are in the natural order of things, therefore, two causes, character and thought, of their actions, and consequently of their success or failure in their lives.

Now the action (that which is done) is represented in the play by the plot. The plot, in our present sense of the term, is simply this, the combination of the incidents; whereas character is what makes us ascribe certain moral qualities to the agents; and thought is shown in all they say when proving a particular point or, it may be, enunciating a general truth.

There are six parts consequently of every tragedy, as a whole, that provides its quality, viz. plot, character, speech, thought, spectacle and music-dance; two of them arising from the means, one from the manner, and three from the objects of the dramatic imitation;

and there is nothing else besides these six. Of these, its formative elements, then, not a few of the dramatists have made due use, as every play, one may say, admits of spectacle, character, plot, speech, music-dance, and thought.

The most important of the six is the combination of the incidents. Tragedy is essentially a representation not of persons but of action and life, of happiness and misery. All human happiness or misery takes the form of action; the end for which we live is a certain kind of activity, not a quality. Character gives us qualities, but it is in our actions—what we do—that we are happy or the reverse. In a play accordingly they do not act in order to portray character; they include character for the sake of the action. So that it is the action in it, i.e. its plot, that is the end and purpose of the tragedy; and the end is everywhere the chief thing.

Besides this, a tragedy is impossible without action, but there may be one without character. The tragedies of most of the moderns are characterless—a defect common among creators of all kinds, and with its counterpart in painting is Zeuxis as compared with Polygnotus; for whereas the latter is strong in character, the work of Zeuxis is devoid of it.

And again: one may string together a series of characteristic speeches of the utmost finish as regards speech and thought, and yet fail to produce the true effect of tragedy; but one will have much better success with a tragedy which, however inferior in these respects, has a plot, a combination of incidents, in it. And again: the most powerful parts of the emotional effect in tragedy, the peripeties [i.e., reversals] and discoveries [which will be discussed in Chapter 11 and 16], are parts of the plot. A further proof is in the fact that beginners succeed earlier with the speech and character than with the arrangement of the incidents; and the same may be said of nearly all the early dramatists.

We maintain, therefore, that the first essential, the life and soul, so to speak, of tragedy is the plot; and that character comes second—compare the parallel in painting, where the most beautiful colors laid on without order will not give one the same pleasure as a simple black-and-white sketch of a portrait. We maintain that tragedy is primarily an impersonation of action, and that it is mainly for the sake of the action that it represents the personal agents.

Third comes the element of thought, i.e. the power of saying whatever can be said, or what is appropriate to the occasion. This is what, in the speeches in tragedy, falls under the arts of politics and rhetoric; for the older dramatists make their personages discourse like statesmen and the moderns like rhetoricians. One must not confuse it with character. Character in a play is that which reveals the moral purpose of the agents, i.e. the sort of thing they seek or avoid, where that is not obvious—hence there is no room for character in a speech on a purely indifferent subject. Thought, on the other hand, is shown in all they say when proving or disproving some particular point, or enunciating some universal proposition.

Fourth is the speech of the personages, i.e., as before explained, the expression of their thoughts in words, which is practically the same thing with verse as with prose.

As for the two remaining parts, the music-dance [primarily the choral art] is the greatest of the pleasurable accessories of tragedy. The spectacle, though an attraction, is the least artistic of all the parts, and has least to do with the art of dramatic musical composition. The power of tragedy is quite possible without a competition and the [special] actors [of the competitions]; and besides, the getting-up of the spectacle is more a matter for the costumier than the composer.

Chapter 7

Having thus distinguished the parts, let us now consider the proper construction of the arrangement of incidents, as that is at once the first and the most important thing in tragedy.

We have laid it down that a tragedy is a representation of an action that is complete in itself, as a whole of some magnitude; for a whole may be of no magnitude to speak of. Now a whole is that which has beginning, middle, and end. A beginning is that which is not itself necessarily after anything else, and which has naturally something else after it; an end is that which is naturally after something itself, either as its necessary or usual consequent, and with nothing else after it; and a middle, that which is by nature after one thing and has also another after it. A well-constructed plot, therefore, cannot either begin or end at any point one likes; beginning and end in it must be of the forms just described.

Again, to be beautiful, a living creature, and every whole made up of parts, must not only present a certain order in its arrangement of parts, but also be of a certain definite magnitude. Beauty is a matter of size and order, and therefore impossible either (1) in a very minute creature, since our perception becomes indistinct as it approaches instantaneity; or (2) in a creature of vast size—one, say, 1,000 miles long—as in that case, instead of the object being seen all at once, the unity and wholeness of it is lost to the beholder.

Just in the same way, then, as a beautiful whole made up of parts, or a beautiful living creature, must be of some size, a size to be taken in by the eye, so a plot must be of some length, but of a length to be taken in by the memory. As for the limit of its length, so far as that is relative to public performances and spectators, it does not fall within the art [of tragedy]. If they had to perform a hundred tragedies, they would be timed by water-clocks, as they are said to have been at one period. The limit, however, set by the actual nature of the thing is this: the longer the action, consistently with its being comprehensible as a whole, the finer it is by reason of its magnitude.

As a rough general formula, a length which allows of the hero passing by a series of probable or necessary stages *from bad fortune to good fortune, or from good to bad,* may suffice as a limit for the magnitude of the story.

Chapter 8

The unity of a plot does not consist, as some suppose, in its having one man as its subject. An infinity of things befall that one man, some of which it is impossible to reduce to unity; and in like manner there are many actions of one man which cannot be made to form one action.

We see, therefore, the mistake of all the composers who have created a *Heracleid*, a *Theseid*, or similar works; they suppose that, because Heracles was one man, the plot also of Heracles must have unity. Homer, however, evidently understood this point quite well, whether by art or instinct, just in the same way as he surpasses the rest in every other respect. In creating an *Odyssey*, he did not make the composition cover all that ever befell his hero—it befell him, for instance, to get wounded on Parnassus and also to feign madness at the time of the call to arms, but the two incidents had no probable or necessary connexion with one another—instead of doing that, he took an action with a unity of the kind we describe as the subject of the *Odyssey*, as also of the *Iliad*.

The truth is that, just as in the other imitative arts one imitation is always of one thing, so the plot, as a representation of action, must represent one action, a complete whole, with its several incidents so closely connected that the transposal or withdrawal of any one of them will disjoin and dislocate the whole. For that which makes no perceptible difference by its presence or absence is no real part of the whole.

Chapter 9

From what we have said it will be seen that the composer's function is to describe, not the thing that has happened, but a kind of thing that might happen, i.e. what is possible as being probable or necessary. The distinction between historian and composer is not in the one writing prose and the other verse—you might put the work of Herodotus into verse, and it would still be a species of history; it consists really in this, that the one describes the thing that has been, and the other a kind of thing that might be. Hence (dramatic) composition is something more philosophic and of graver import than history, since its statements are of the nature rather of universals, whereas those of history are singulars.

By a universal statement I mean one as to what such or such a kind of man will probably or necessarily say or do—which is the aim of dramatic composition, though it affixes proper names to the characters; by a singular statement, one as to what, say, Alcibiades did or had done to him. In comedy this has become clear by this time; it is only when their plot is already made up of probable incidents that they give it a basis of proper names, choosing for the purpose any names that may occur to them, instead of creating like the old iambic composers about particular persons.

In tragedy, however, they still adhere to the historic names; and for this reason: what convinces is the possible; now, whereas we are not yet sure as to the possibility of that which has not happened, that which has happened is manifestly possible, else it would not have come to pass. Nevertheless even in tragedy there are some plays with but one or two known names in them, the rest being inventions; and there are some without a single known name, e.g. Agathon's *Antheus*, in which both incidents and names are of the dramatist's invention; and it is no less delightful on that account.

So one must not aim at a rigid adherence to the traditional stories on which tragedies are based. It would be absurd, in fact, to do so, as even the known stories are only known to a few, though they are a delight nonetheless to all.

It is evident from the above that the dramatist must be more the maker of his plots than of his verses, inasmuch as he is a dramatist by virtue of the representative element in his work, and it is actions that he represents. And if he should come to take a subject from actual history, he is none the less a dramatist for that; since some historic occurrences may very well be in the [kind of] probable and possible order of things [that could occur again]; and it is in that aspect of them that he is their dramatist.

Of simple plots and actions the episodic are the worst. I call a plot episodic when there is neither probability nor necessity in the sequence of episodes. Actions of this sort bad composers construct through their own fault, and good ones on account of the actors. His work being for public performance, a good composer often stretches out a plot beyond its capabilities, and is thus obliged to twist the sequence of incidents.

Tragedy, however, is an impersonation not only of a complete action, but also of incidents arousing pity and fear.[14] Such incidents have the very greatest effect

---

14 Although this strikes some as the first legitimate use of pity and fear in the treatise, it is quite possible that the phrase with "pity and fear" was interpolated here, too, to fill a gap in the original corrupted manuscript, whether literal or conceptual. That is, the subsequent explanation does *not* involve pity and fear, but the marvelous, which we will see in later chapters is undoubtedly a major concern for Aristotle.

on the mind when they occur unexpectedly and at the same time in consequence of one another; there is more of the marvellous in them then than if they happened of themselves or by mere chance. Even matters of chance seem most marvellous if there is an appearance of design as it were in them; as for instance the statue of Mitys at Argos killed the author of Mitys' death by falling down on him when a looker-on at a public spectacle; for incidents like that we think to be not without a meaning. A plot, therefore, of this sort is necessarily finer than others.

Chapter 10

Plots are either simple or complex, since the actions they represent are naturally of this twofold description. The action, proceeding in the way defined, as one continuous whole, I call simple, when the change in the hero's fortunes takes place without peripety or discovery; and complex, when it involves one or the other or both. These should each of them arise out of the structure of the plot itself, so as to be the consequence, necessary or probable, of the antecedents. There is a great difference between a thing happening *because* of something and merely *after* something.

Chapter 11

A peripety is the change from one state of things within the play to its opposite of the kind described, and that too in the way we are saying, in the probable or necessary sequence of events; as it is for instance in *Oedipus*: here the opposite state of things is produced by the Messenger, who, coming to gladden Oedipus and to remove his fears as to his mother, reveals the secret of his birth. And in *Lynceus*: just as he is being led off for execution, with Danaus at his side to put him to death, the incidents preceding this bring it about that he is saved and Danaus put to death.[15]

A discovery is, as the very word implies, a change from ignorance to knowledge, and thus to either love or hate, in the personages marked for good or evil fortune. The finest form of discovery is one attended by peripeties, like that which goes with the discovery in *Oedipus*. There are no doubt other forms of it; what we have said may happen in a way in reference to inanimate things, even things of a very casual kind; and it is also possible to discover whether someone has done or not done something. But the form most directly connected with the plot and the action of the piece is the first-mentioned. This, with a peripety, will arouse

---

15 The lost *Lynceus* is by Aristotle's friend, the rhetorician and tragedian Theodectes (ca. 400-334). The play dealt with the daughters of King Danaus of Argos, who ordered them to murder their new husbands. Only Hypermestra dared disobey and spare her husband Lynceus. She gave birth to a boy, and when Danaus became aware of the child he demanded Lynceus's death. As a result of an unknown sequence of events Danaus died himself, and thus the play ends happily. (I owe this background to Janko.)

either pity or fear—actions of that nature being what tragedy is assumed to represent; and it will also serve to bring about *the happy* or unhappy ending.[16] The discovery, then, being of persons, it may be that of one party only to the other, the latter being already known; or both the parties may have to discover themselves. Iphigenia, for instance, was discovered to Orestes by sending the letter; and another discovery was required to reveal him to Iphigenia.[17]

Two parts of the plot, then, peripety and discovery, are on matters of this sort. A third part is suffering; which we may define as an action of a destructive or painful nature, such as murders on the stage, tortures, woundings, and the like. The other two have been already explained.

---

16 Again, the insertion of pity and fear seems utterly mechanical and disconnected from the rest of the chapter. Why does a peripety arouse pity or fear when it brings about the *happy* ending? We can remove the clause with pity and fear and Aristotle's ideas are tighter and more consistent. Moreover, it is then also consistent with Chapter 6 in which the peripeties and discoveries are said to be part of the plot and to give, *not* pity and fear, but the strongest emotional effect, cashed out there as *pleasure* in the explanation that employs random colors versus drawings as an analogue.

17 This appears to be the version of *Iphigenia (in Tauris)* that ends happily, as mentioned later in Chapter 14 when Aristotle ranks those plays highest, even above *Oedipus*.

Chapter 12

The parts of tragedy to be treated as formative [that is, "qualitative"] elements in the whole were mentioned in a previous chapter [namely, Chapter 6].

From the point of view, however, of its quantity, i.e. the separate sections into which it is divided, a tragedy has the following parts: Prologue, Episode, Exode, and a choral portion, distinguished into Parode and Stasimon; *these two are common to all tragedies*, whereas songs from the stage and 'commoi' are only found in some [which is why *melopoiia* may include the latter but primarily means the choral art in Chapter 6].

The Prologue is all that precedes the Parode of the chorus; an Episode all that comes in between two whole choral music-dances; the Exode all that follows after the last choral music-dance. In the choral portion the Parode is the whole first speech of the chorus; a Stasimon, a song and dance of the chorus without anapaests or trochees; a 'commos', a lamentation by chorus and actors in concert.

[Again:] The parts of tragedy to be used as formative elements in the whole we have already mentioned; the above are its parts from the point of view of its quantity, or the separate sections into which it is divided.

Chapter 13

The next points after what we have said above will be these: (1) What is the dramatist to aim at, and what is he to avoid, in constructing his plots? and (2) What are the conditions on which the effect of tragedy depends?

We assume that, for the finest form of tragedy, the plot must be not simple but complex; and further, that it must represent actions arousing pity and fear, since that is the distinctive function of *this* kind of impersonation.[18] It follows, therefore, that there are three forms of plot to be avoided.

(1) A good man must not be seen passing from happiness to misery, or (2) a bad man from misery to happiness. The first situation is not fear-inspiring or piteous, but simply odious to us. The second is the most untragic that can be; it has none of the requisites of [this kind of] tragedy; it does not appeal either to the human feeling in us, or to our pity, or to our fears. Nor, on the other hand, should (3) an *extremely* bad man be seen falling from happiness into misery. Such a story may arouse the human feeling in us, but it will not move us to either pity or fear; pity is occasioned by undeserved misfortune, and fear by that of one like

---

18 This is arguably the first authentic mention of pity and fear, given the associated discussion in the rest of the chapter. The reason, as explained thoroughly in *ADMC*, is that Aristotle has decided to focus on a *subset* of tragedy that ends unhappily. More on this in Chapters 14A and 18.

ourselves; so that there will be nothing either piteous or fear-inspiring in the situation.

There remains, then, the intermediate kind of personage, a man not pre-eminently virtuous and just, whose misfortune, however, is brought upon him not by vice and depravity but by some error of judgement, of the number of those in the enjoyment of great reputation and prosperity; e.g. Oedipus, Thyestes, and the men of note of similar families.

The perfect plot, accordingly, must have a single, and not (as some tell us) a double issue; the change in the hero's fortunes must be not from misery to happiness, but on the contrary from happiness to misery; and the cause of it must lie not in any depravity, but in some great error on his part; the man himself being either such as we have described, or better, not worse, than that.

Fact also confirms our theory. Though the poets began by accepting any story that came to hand, in these days the finest tragedies are always on the story of some few houses, on that of Alcmeon, Oedipus, Orestes, Meleager, Thyestes, Telephus, or any others that may have been involved, as either agents or sufferers, in some deed of horror. The theoretically best tragedy, then, has a plot of this description. The critics, therefore, are wrong who blame Euripides for taking this line in his tragedies, and giving many of them an unhappy ending. It is, as we have said, the right line to take. The best proof is this: on the stage, that is, in the competitions, such plays, properly worked out, are seen to be the most truly tragic; and Euripides, even if his management be faulty in other respects, is seen to be nevertheless the most tragic of the dramatists.

After this comes the construction of plot which some rank first, one with a double story (like the *Odyssey*) and an opposite issue for the good and the bad personages. It is ranked as first only through the weakness of the audiences; the dramatists merely follow their public, creating as its wishes dictate. But the pleasure here is not that of tragedy. It belongs more to comedy, where the bitterest enemies in the piece (e.g. Orestes and Aegisthus) walk off good friends at the end, with no slaying of any one by any one.

Chapter 14A

The fear and pity may be aroused by the spectacle; but they may also be aroused by the very structure and incidents of the play—which is the better way and shows the better dramatist. The plot in fact should be so framed that, even without seeing the things take place, he who simply hears the account of them shall be filled with horror and pity at the incidents; which is just the effect that the mere recital of the story in *Oedipus* would have on one. To produce this same effect by means of the spectacle is less artistic, and requires extraneous aid. Those, however, who make use of the spectacle to put before us that which is merely monstrous and not productive of fear, are wholly out of touch with tragedy; not every kind of pleasure should be required of a tragedy, but only its own proper pleasure.

Since the dramatist has to produce the [proper] pleasure through impersonation from [the type of play that also has] pity and fear, it is clear that the causes should be included in the incidents of his story.[19] Let us see, then, what kinds of incident strike one as horrible, or rather as piteous. In a deed of this description the parties must necessarily be either friends, or enemies, or indifferent to one another. Now when enemy does it on enemy, there is nothing to move us to pity either in his doing or in his meditating the deed, except so far as the actual pain of the sufferer is concerned; and the same is true when the parties are indifferent to one another. Whenever the tragic deed, however, is done within the family—when murder or the like is done or meditated by brother on brother, by son on father, by mother on son, or son on mother—these are the situations the dramatist should seek after.

---

19 This is one of the most difficult and important statements of the book. It is important because catharsis is completely missing and pleasure emphasized, which accords with my interpretation. It is difficult because the Greek is short and the pleasure comes "from" (*apo*) the pity and fear, as every translator to my knowledge keeps. Yet *Rhetoric* II 5 and 8 clearly state pity and fear are painful emotions. Thus, unless Aristotle were (absurdly) requiring psychological masochism, the statement must be elliptical or the passage was corrupted, and I give one option to make sense of it.

DRAMATICS

Chapter 14B [20]

The traditional stories, accordingly, must be kept as they are, e.g. the murder of Clytaemnestra by Orestes and of Eriphyle by Alcmeon. At the same time even with these there is something left to the dramatist himself; it is for him to devise the right way of treating them. Let us explain more clearly what we mean by 'the right way'.

The deed of horror may be done by the doer knowingly and consciously, as in the old creators, and in Medea's murder of her children in Euripides.

Or he may do it, but in ignorance of his relationship, and discover that afterwards, as does the *Oedipus* in Sophocles. Here the deed is outside the play; but it may be within it, like the act of Astydamas's *Alcmeon* or that of Telegonus in *Ulysses Wounded*.

---

20 The chapter divisions were a product not of Aristotle but of the early Renaissance. André Dacier (1651–1722), one of the great translators and commentators, broke Chapter 14 instead into two, ending with 27 chapters. I divide it at a different spot but keep the number so that there is a numerical correspondence with the traditional chapters apart from Dacier. Given that pity and fear play no role in this section, given that Aristotle in no way refers back to his positions in Chapter 13, and given that the ranking of serious drama is different from Chapter 13, either Chapter 14B was from another text of Aristotle, dealing with tragedy in general, or we are missing a substantial part of the manuscripts in which the subset of plays with pity and fear are distinguished from the other types of plays. More on this in Chapter 18.

A third possibility is for one meditating some deadly injury to another, in ignorance of his relationship, to make the discovery in time to draw back.

These exhaust the possibilities, since the deed must necessarily be either done or not done, and either knowingly or unknowingly.[21]

> (i) The worst situation is when the personage is with full knowledge on the point of doing the deed, and leaves it undone. It is odious and also (through the absence of suffering) untragic; hence it is that no one is made to act thus except in some few instances, e.g. Haemon and Creon in *Antigone*.[22]

---

21 One puzzle that commentators have had is Aristotle describing briefly only three of the possible four options before making the statement implying that these are the (four) possibilities. However, if the Northern Greek can mean by "these" the four options that he then subsequently and immediately explains, there is no problem. This would be especially plausible were Aristotle using a diagram simultaneously; see Carlo Natali, *Aristotle: His Life and School*, ed. by D.S. Hutchinson (Princeton: Princeton University Press, 2013).

22 To my knowledge, every previous commentator assumes that this is the *Antigone* of Sophocles, which, however is very tragic, with multiple suicides. In *Aristotle's Favorite Tragedy: Oedipus or Cresphontes?, op. cit.*, I provide the arguments and evidence that it must be instead the *Antigone* of Euripides, which ends happily, but which, *in revising drastically the traditional myth*, breaks the rule that Aristotle has noted at the very beginning of Chapter 14B and is therefore odious (or shocking, another meaning of *miaros*).

(ii) Next after this comes the actual perpetration of the deed meditated.

(iii) A better situation than that, however, is for the deed to be done in ignorance, and the relationship discovered afterwards, since there is nothing odious in it, and the discovery will serve to astound us.[23]

(iv) But the best of all is the last; what we have in *Cresphontes*, for example, where Merope, on the point of slaying her son, recognizes him in time; in *Iphigenia*, where sister and brother are in a like position; and in *Helle*, where the son recognizes his mother, when on the point of giving her up to her enemy.

This will explain why our tragedies are restricted (as we said above) to such a small number of families.[24]

---

23 This recapitulates the example of *Oedipus* from a few paragraphs back. *Medea* exemplifies (ii) there.

24 The astute reader will wonder *how* the best tragedies ending happily explains why tragedies are restricted to a small number of families. Fyfe suggests that Aristotle is referring back to Chapter 13, namely, "the finest tragedies are always on the story of some few houses, on that of Alcmeon, Oedipus, Orestes ... or any others that may have been involved, as either agents or sufferers, in some deed of horror." This is extremely baffling because the *deed* of horror is averted in *Cresphontes et al* (although there may have been the *threat* of the deed, which is a very different matter). Recall also that in Chapter 9 the plots need not be based on a few houses, and Agathon created the *Antheus,* "in which both incidents and names are of the dramatist's invention; and it is no less delightful on that account."

It was accident rather than art that led the dramatists in quest of subjects to embody this kind of incident in their plots. They are still obliged, accordingly, to have recourse to the families in which such horrors have occurred.

On the construction of the plot, and the kind of plot required for tragedy, enough has now been said.[25]

Chapter 15

Regarding character, there are four points to aim at. First and foremost, the characters shall be good.[26] There will be an element of character in the play, if (as has been observed) what a personage says or does reveals a certain moral purpose; and a good element

---

Either, then, this passage in 14B is out of place or there is some other explanation, but, again, we have evidence that the treatise is an amalgamation or has many lost sections.

25 Given this statement, and Aristotle switching in the next chapter to a discussion of character, the second most important necessary condition of Chapter 6, it is extremely probable that Chapters 17 and 18, also on plot, were from a different treatment and were interpolated into the manuscripts we possess. Other reasons for this conclusion appear at the end of Chapter 15 and in Chapters 17 and 18 themselves.

26 This statement shows that, much as the Northern Greek may disagree at times with his mentor Plato, and much as scholars have argued for generations that the *Dramatics* is a response to Plato's censorship of tragedy and comedy, as found especially in the *Republic*, Aristotle clearly is Platonic in some ways when it comes to drama.

of character, if the purpose so revealed is good. Such goodness is possible in every type of personage, even in a woman or a slave, though the one is perhaps an inferior, and the other a wholly worthless being.

The second point is to make them appropriate. The character before us may be, say, manly; but it is not appropriate in a female character to be manly or clever.

The third is to make them like the reality, which is not the same as their being good and appropriate, in our sense of the term.

The fourth is to make them consistent and the same throughout; even if inconsistency be part of the man before one for impersonation as presenting that form of character, he should still be consistently inconsistent.

We have an instance of baseness of character, not required for the story, in the Menelaus in *Orestes*; of the incongruous and unbefitting in the lamentation of Ulysses in *Scylla*, and in the (clever) speech of Melanippe; and of inconsistency in *Iphigenia at Aulis*, where Iphigenia the suppliant is utterly unlike the later Iphigenia.

The right thing, however, about character, just as in the incidents of the play, is to endeavour always after the necessary or the probable; so that whenever such-and-such a personage says or does such-and-such a thing, it shall be the probable or necessary outcome of his character; and whenever this incident follows on that, it shall be either the necessary or the probable consequence of it.

From this one sees (to digress for a moment) that the denouement also should arise out of the plot itself, and not depend on a stage-artifice, as in *Medea*, or in the story of the (arrested) departure of the Greeks in the *Iliad*.

The artifice must be reserved for matters outside the play—for past events beyond human knowledge, or events yet to come, which need to be foretold or announced; since it is the privilege of the gods to know everything. There should be nothing improbable among the actual incidents. If it be unavoidable, however, it should be outside the tragedy, like the improbability in the *Oedipus* of Sophocles.

Because tragedy is a representation of personages better than the ordinary man, we in our way should follow the example of good portrait-painters, who reproduce the distinctive features of a man, and at the same time, without losing the likeness, make him handsomer than he is. The dramatist in like manner, in portraying men quick or slow to anger, or with similar infirmities of character, must know how to represent them as such, and at the same time as good men, as Agathon and Homer have represented Achilles.

All these rules one must keep in mind throughout,

and further, *those also for such points of stage-effect as directly depend on the art of the dramatist*, since in these too one may often make mistakes. Enough, however, has been said on the subject in one of our published writings.[27]

Chapter 16

Discovery in general has been explained already [in Chapter 11].

As for the species of discovery, the first to be noted is (1) the least artistic form of it, of which the tragedians make most use through mere lack of invention, discovery by signs or marks. Of these signs some are congenital, like the 'lance-head which the Earth-born have on them', or 'stars', such as Carcinus incorporates in his *Thyestes*; others acquired after birth—these latter being either marks on the body, e.g. scars, or external tokens, like necklaces, or to take another sort of instance, the ark in the discovery in *Tyro*. Even these, however, admit of two uses, a better and a

---

27 The same subject is taken up in Chapter 17, which suggests that Chapter 17 was (at least part of) the published writings. The Northern Greek establishes a pattern now that he continues in Chapter 19 when he discusses there the third most important necessary condition of tragedy from Chapter 6, *dianoia* ("thought" or "reasoning"): In Chapter 19 he says enough has been said about *dianoia* in his *Rhetoric*, with the strong suggestion that the reader go look at that treatise for more details.

worse: the scar of Ulysses is an instance; the discovery of him through it is made in one way by the nurse and in another by the swineherds. A discovery using signs as a means of assurance is less artistic, as indeed are all such as imply reflection; whereas one bringing them in all of a sudden, as in the *Bath-story*, is of a better order.

Next after these are (2) discoveries made directly by the tragedian; which are inartistic for that very reason; e.g. Orestes's discovery of himself in *Iphigenia*: whereas his sister reveals who she is by the letter, Orestes is made to say himself what the dramatist rather than the story demands. This, therefore, is not far removed from the first-mentioned fault, since he might have presented certain tokens as well. Another instance is the 'shuttle's voice' in the *Tereus* of Sophocles.

(3) A third species is discovery through memory, from a man's consciousness being awakened by something seen or heard. Thus in *The Cyprioe* of Dicaeogenes, the sight of the picture makes the man burst into tears; and in the *Tale of Alcinous*, hearing the harper, Ulysses is reminded of the past and weeps; the discovery of them being the result.

(4) A fourth kind is discovery through reasoning; e.g. in *The Choephoroe*: 'One like me is here; there is no one like me but Orestes; he, therefore, must be here.' Or that which Polyidus the Sophist suggested for *Iphigenia*; since it was natural for Orestes to reflect:

'My sister was sacrificed, and I am to be sacrificed like her.' Or that in the *Tydeus* of Theodectes: 'I came to find a son, and am to die myself.' Or that in *The Phinidae*: on seeing the place the women inferred their fate, that they were to die there, since they had also been exposed there.

(5) There is, too, a composite discovery arising from bad reasoning on the side of the other party. An instance of it is in *Ulysses the False Messenger*: he said he should know the bow—which he had not seen; but to suppose from that that he would know it again (as though he had once seen it) was bad reasoning.

(6) The best of all discoveries, however, is that arising from the incidents themselves, when the great surprise comes about through a probable incident, like that in the *Oedipus* of Sophocles; and also in *Iphigenia*; for it was not improbable that she should wish to have a letter taken home. These last are the only discoveries independent of the artifice of signs and necklaces. Next [in reverse order of importance] after them come discoveries through reasoning.

Chapter 17 [28]

At the time when he is constructing his plots, and engaged on the speech in which they are worked out, the tragedian should remember (1) to put the actual scenes as far as possible before his eyes. In this way, seeing everything with the vividness of an eye-witness, as it were, he will devise what is appropriate and be least likely to overlook incongruities. This is shown by what was censured in Carcinus, the return of Amphiaraus from the sanctuary; it would have passed unnoticed, if it had not been actually seen by the audience; but on the stage his play failed, the incongruity of the incident offending the spectators.

(2) As far as may be, too, the tragedian should even act his story with the very gestures of his personages. Given the same natural qualifications, he who feels the emotions to be described will be the most convincing; distress and anger, for instance, are portrayed most truthfully by one who is feeling them at the moment. Hence it is that dramatic composition demands a man with special gift for it, or else one with a touch of madness in him; the former can easily assume the required mood, and the latter may be actually beside himself

---

[28] As noted, this chapter is arguably referred to at the end of Chapter 15, as a "published" text, which would mean that it was written before our *Dramatics*. Still, it seems consistent with the previous chapters, one major reason a later editor had no qualms about interpolating it, even though it is about plot and even though the end of Chapter 14 indicates that the Stagirite is finished with plot.

with emotion.

(3) His story, again, whether already made or of his own making, he should first simplify and reduce to a universal form, before proceeding to lengthen it out by the insertion of episodes. The following will show how the universal element in *Iphigenia*, for instance, may be viewed: A certain maiden having been offered in sacrifice, and spirited away from her sacrificers into another land, where the custom was to sacrifice all strangers to the Goddess, she was made there the priestess of this rite. Long after that the brother of the priestess happened to come; the fact, however, of the oracle having for a certain reason bidden him go thither, and his object in going, are outside the plot of the play. On his coming he was arrested, and about to be sacrificed, when he revealed who he was—either as Euripides puts it, or (as suggested by Polyidus) by the not improbable exclamation, 'So I too am doomed to be sacrificed, as my sister was'; and the disclosure led to his salvation.

This done, the next thing, after the proper names have been fixed as a basis for the story, is to work in episodes or accessory incidents. One must mind, however, that the episodes are appropriate, like the fit of madness in Orestes, which led to his arrest, and the purifying, which brought about his salvation. In plays, then, the episodes are short; in epic composition they serve to lengthen out the work. The synopsis of the *Odyssey* is not a long one. A certain man has been abroad many years; Poseidon is ever on the watch for him, and he is all alone. Matters at home too have come to this, that his substance is being wasted and his son's death plotted by suitors to his wife. Then he arrives there himself after his grievous sufferings; reveals himself, and falls on his enemies; and the end is his salvation and their death. This being all that is proper to the *Odyssey*, everything else in it is episode.

Chapter 18

There is a further point to be borne in mind. Every tragedy is in part complication and in part denouement; the incidents before the opening scene, and often certain also of those within the play, forming the complication; and the rest the denouement. By complication I mean all from the beginning of the story to the point just before the change in the hero's fortunes; by denouement, all from the beginning of the change to the end. In the *Lynceus* of Theodectes, for instance, the complication includes, together with the presupposed incidents, the seizure of the child and that in turn of the parents; and the denouement all from the indictment for the murder to the end. Now it is right, when one speaks of a tragedy as the same or not the same as another, to do so on the ground before all else of their plot, i.e. as having the same or not the same complication and denouement. Yet there are many tragedians who, after a good complication, fail in the denouement. But it is necessary for both points of construction to be always duly mastered.

There are four distinct species of tragedy—that being the number of the constituents also that have been mentioned[29]: first, the complex tragedy, which is all peripety and discovery; second, the tragedy of suffering, e.g. the *Ajaxes* and *Ixions*; third, the tragedy of character, e.g. *The Phthian Women* and *Peleus*. The fourth constituent is that of spectacle,[30] exemplified in *The Phorcides*, in *Prometheus*, and in all plays with the scene laid in the nether-world. The dramatist's aim, then, should be to combine every element of interest, if possible, or else the more important and the major part of them. This is now especially necessary owing to the unfair criticism to which the tragedian is subjected in these days. Just because there have been dramatists before him strong in the several species of tragedy, the critics now expect the one man to surpass that which

---

29 This comment suggests that this chapter is not from the original *Dramatics*. Nowhere are four constituents given and, rather, in Chapter 6 *six* necessary conditions that all tragedies have are explained. Also, two of the upcoming species—"tragedy of suffering" and "tragedy of character"— have never been introduced and will never be mentioned elsewhere in the book. Alternatively, *extensive* passages on tragedy (and not only comedy) were lost.

30 The Greek is corrupted here. Some scholars have guessed that "simple" (in contrast to "complex") tragedy is meant. It is impossible to determine for sure but one argument for "simple" is that later in the chapter the Northern Greek contrasts "complex" and "simple." Also, in Chapter 24 he says that epic has the same number of species as tragedy and he gives "complex" and "simple."

was the strong point of each one of his predecessors.

One should also remember what has been said more than once, and not write a tragedy on an epic body of incidents (i.e. one with a plurality of stories in it), by attempting to dramatize, for instance, the entire story of the *Iliad*. In the epic owing to its scale every part is treated at proper length; with a drama, however, on the same story the result is very disappointing. This is shown by the fact that all who have dramatized the fall of Ilium in its entirety, and not part by part, like Euripides, or the whole of the Niobe story, instead of a portion, like Aeschylus, either fail utterly or have but ill success on the stage; for that and that alone was enough to ruin a play by Agathon.

Yet in their peripeties, as also in their simple plots, the dramatists I mean show wonderful skill in aiming at the kind of effect they desire—a tragic situation that arouses the human feeling in one, like the clever villain (e.g. Sisyphus) deceived, or the brave wrongdoer worsted. This is probable, however, only in Agathon's sense, when he speaks of the probability of even improbabilities coming to pass.

The chorus too should be regarded as one of the actors; it should be an integral part of the whole, and take a share in the action—that which it has in Sophocles rather than in Euripides. With the later tragedians, however, the songs in a play of theirs have no more to do with the plot of that than of any other tragedy.

Hence it is that they are now singing intercalary pieces, a practice first introduced by Agathon. And yet what real difference is there between singing such intercalary pieces, and attempting to fit in a speech, or even a whole act, from one play into another?

Chapter 19

Plot and character having been discussed, it remains to consider the speech and thought. As for thought, we may assume what is said of it in our *Art of Rhetoric*, as it belongs more properly to that department of inquiry. The thought of the personages is shown in everything to be effected by their language—in every effort to prove or disprove, to arouse emotion (pity, fear, anger, and the like), or to maximize or minimize things. It is clear, also, that their mental procedure must be on the same lines in their actions likewise, whenever they wish them to arouse pity or horror, or have a look of importance or probability. The only difference is that with the act [on stage] the impression has to be made without explanation; whereas with the spoken word it has to be produced by the speaker, and result from his language. What, indeed, would be the good of the speaker, if things appeared in the required light even apart from anything he says?

As regards the speech, one subject for inquiry under this head is the turns given to the language when spoken; e.g. the difference between command and prayer, simple statement and threat, question and answer, and so forth. *The theory of such matters, however, belongs to elocution and the professors of that art.* Whether the dramatist knows these things or not, his art as a composer is never seriously criticized on that account. What fault can one see in Homer's 'Sing of the wrath, Goddess'?—which Protagoras has criticized as being a command where a prayer was meant, since to bid one do or not do, he tells us, is a command. *Let us pass over this, then, as appertaining to another art, and not to that of dramatic composition.*

Chapter 20

[Translator's Comment: Especially given the statements in Chapter 19, in which the theory of language is relegated to another field, it is inconceivable to me that Aristotle would have concerned himself with basic grammar and basic theory of language in a book on dramatic musical composition. Following the principle enunciated in the Introduction, I keep Chapters 20-22 here, but the likeliest scenario, given my arguments in previous books, is that the sections on metaphor may be legitimate and that some of the passages on metaphor in the *Rhetoric* III were originally at this location instead.[31] In any event, those interested in the details of language might find here many points of great value, and Chapter 22 has references to tragedians, epic and iambic composers, all the art forms that Aristotle have mentioned repeatedly throughout this book.

---

31 Cf. *Rhetoric* III 2-11; also see my *A Primer on Aristotle's DRAMATICS*, pp. 82; 204; 207-9; 211; and 291.

DRAMATICS

The unusual aspect in the *Rhetoric*, which to my knowledge no one addresses, is that metaphor is said by the Northern Greek to be more applicable to prose than to verse and that simile is more relevant to verse, and yet we have nothing in this treatise on simile.[32] All ancient Greek drama (at least until Aristotle) used verse rather than prose. Why, then, would he concentrate on metaphor in a section on language *qua* verse rather than just mention some general principles?

These chapters are no different from Bywater's original, except for "composer" usually in lieu of "poet," and "dramatic composition" for "poetry," since the examples may have come (and in the examples of Cleophon and Sthenelus did come) in the context of dramatic musical works and "composer" will cover both, although "poet" misleads. Moreover, as in Chapter 19, "language" or "speech" is used in lieu of the unduly restrictive translation of "diction," which other translators have used but which for modern English speakers typically has a very narrow meaning of enunciation or choice of vocabulary. Obviously, given the broad issues, Aristotle is not focussing on such a narrow aspect of language here.

---

32 In the *Rhetoric* III 2 Aristotle says that in *peri poiētikēs* he gives a classification of metaphors and "mention of the fact metaphor is of great value both in poetry *and in prose*" (*Rhetoric* III 2, 1405a4-7; my italics; transl. W. Rhys Roberts in *The Complete Works of Aristotle,* ed. J. Barnes, *op. cit.,* as are all passages from the *Rhetoric*). He suggests immediately, however, that *prose* writers have to pay more attention to metaphor than *verse* writers and then spends nine more chapters on related issues, often classifying metaphor. For instance, he says at *Rhetoric* III 11, 1411a1 "of the four kinds of metaphor the most taking is the proportional kind," and he repeats what he had said earlier, that *a simile is a kind of metaphor.* Similes had been stressed in *Rhetoric* III 4 to be "*useful in prose as well as in verse; but not often since they are of the nature of poetry*" (1406b24-6; my italics). Simile is never mentioned in our *Dramatics* but is given a chapter in the *Rhetoric*, namely III 4.

The *Rhetoric* also points to the topic of "avoiding meanness (of language)," so Chapter 22, which discusses briefly the topic, may indeed be legitimate, or there was another treatise with a similar name and a similar treatment by Aristotle, or, as noted, passages were combined from different papyri by later editors, probably the ones hired by Apellicon to remedy the damage done to the various manuscripts at Scepsis. [33]]

The language viewed as a whole is made up of the following parts: the Letter (or ultimate element), the Syllable, the Conjunction, the Article, the Noun, the Verb, the Case, and the Speech.

(1) The Letter is an indivisible sound of a particular kind, one that may become a factor in an intelligible sound. Indivisible sounds are uttered by the brutes also, but no one of these is a Letter in our sense of the term. These elementary sounds are either vowels, semivowels, or mutes. A vowel is a Letter having an audible sound without the addition of another Letter. A semivowel, one having an audible sound by the addition of another Letter; e.g. S and R. A mute, one having no sound at all by itself, but becoming audible by an addition, that of one of the Letters which have

---

33 See my *A Primer on Aristotle's DRAMATICS, op. cit.*, Appendix 2, for a detailed evaluation of the reports of Strabo, Posidonius, and Plutarch of Aristotle's library being taken to this town in modern northwest Turkey by Neleus, to whom Theophrastus, Aristotle's heir, had bequeathed it. As alluded to, Neleus's own heirs then buried the library in a trench or cellar to hide it from the book-robbing kings of nearby Pergamum, where it was damaged by bugs and moisture. The library was purchased eventually by Apellicon around 130 BCE to make money after restoring it.

a sound of some sort of their own; e.g. D and G. The Letters differ in various ways: as produced by different conformations or in different regions of the mouth; as aspirated, not aspirated, or sometimes one and sometimes the other; as long, short, or of variable quantity; and further as having an acute grave, or intermediate accent. The details of these matters we must leave to the metricians.

(2) A Syllable is a nonsignificant composite sound, made up of a mute and a Letter having a sound (a vowel or semivowel); for GR, without an A, is just as much a Syllable as GRA, with an A. The various forms of the Syllable also belong to the theory of metre.

(3) A Conjunction is (a) a non-significant sound which, when one significant sound is formable out of several, neither hinders nor aids the union, and which, if the Speech thus formed stands by itself (apart from other Speeches) must not be inserted at the beginning of it; e.g. *men, toi, de*. Or (b) a non-significant sound capable of combining two or more significant sounds into one; e.g. *amphi, peri*.

(4) An Article is a non-significant sound marking the beginning, end, or dividing-point of a Speech, its natural place being either at the extremities or in the middle.

(5) A Noun or name is a composite significant sound not involving the idea of time, with parts which have no

significance by themselves in it. It is to be remembered that in a compound we do not think of the parts as having a significance also by themselves; in the name 'Theodorus', for instance, the *dōron* means nothing to us [despite being an inflected variation of "dorus"].

(6) A Verb is a composite significant sound involving the idea of time, with parts which (just as in the Noun) have no significance by themselves in it. Whereas the word 'man' or 'white' does not imply when, 'walks' and 'has walked' involve in addition to the idea of walking that of time present or time past.

(7) A Case of a Noun or Verb is when the word means 'of' or 'to' a thing, and so forth, or for one or many (e.g. 'man' and 'men'); or it may consist merely in the mode of utterance, e.g. in question, command, etc. 'Walked?' and 'Walk!' are Cases of the verb 'to walk' of this last kind.[34]

(8) A Speech is a composite significant sound, some of the parts of which have a certain significance by themselves. It may be observed that a Speech is not always made up of Noun and Verb; it may be without a Verb, like the definition of man; but it will always have some part with a certain significance by itself. In the Speech 'Cleon walks', 'Cleon' is an instance of such a part. A

---

[34] The example of a command is exactly the example that Aristotle says at the end of Chapter 19 we should leave to another art, whether we translate *poiēsis* as "poetry" or "dramatic musical composition."

Speech is said to be one in two ways, either as signifying one thing, or as a union of several Speeches made into one by conjunction. Thus the *Iliad* is one Speech by conjunction of several; and the definition of man is one through its signifying one thing.

Chapter 21

Nouns are of two kinds, either (1) simple, i.e. made up of non-significant parts, like the word *gē*, or (2) double; in the latter case the word may be made up either of a significant and a non-significant part (a distinction which disappears in the compound), or of two significant parts. It is possible also to have triple, quadruple or higher compounds, like most of our amplified names; e.g. 'Hermocaicoxanthus' and the like.

Whatever its structure, a Noun must always be either (1) the ordinary word for the thing, or (2) a strange word, or (3) a metaphor, or (4) an ornamental word, or (5) a coined word, or (6) a word lengthened out, or (7) curtailed, or (8) altered in form. By the ordinary word I mean that in general use in a country; and by a strange word, one in use elsewhere. So that the same word may obviously be at once strange and ordinary, though not in reference to the same people; *sigunon*, for instance, is an ordinary word in Cyprus and a strange word with us.

Metaphor consists in giving the thing a name that

belongs to something else; the transference being either from genus to species, or from species to genus, or from species to species, or on grounds of analogy.

That from genus to species is exemplified in 'Here stands my ship'; for lying at anchor is the 'standing' of a particular kind of thing. That from species to genus in 'Truly ten thousand good deeds has Ulysses wrought', where 'ten thousand', which is a particular large number, is put in place of the generic 'a large number'. That from species to species in 'Drawing the life with the bronze', and in 'Severing with the enduring bronze'; where 'draw' is used in the sense of 'sever' and 'sever' in that of 'draw', both words meaning to 'take away' something.

That from analogy is possible whenever there are four terms so related that the second (B) is to the first (A), as the fourth (D) to the third (C); for one may then metaphorically put B in lieu of D, and D in lieu of B. Now and then, too, they qualify the metaphor by adding on to it that to which the word it supplants is relative. Thus a cup (B) is in relation to Dionysus (A) what a shield (D) is to Ares (C). The cup accordingly will be metaphorically described as the 'shield *of Dionysus*' (D + A), and the shield as the 'cup *of Ares*' (B + C). Or to take another instance: As old age (D) is to life (C), so is evening (B) to day (A). One will accordingly describe evening (B) as the 'old age *of the day*' (D + A)—or by the Empedoclean equivalent; and old age (D) as the 'evening' or 'sunset of life' (B + C).

It may be that some of the terms thus related have no special name of their own, but for all that they will be metaphorically described in just the same way. Thus to cast forth seed-corn is called 'sowing'; but to cast forth its flame, as said of the sun, has no special name. This nameless act (B), however, stands in just the same relation to its object, sunlight (A), as sowing (D) to the seed-corn (C). Hence the expression 'sowing around a god-created *flame*' (D + A).

There is also another form of qualified metaphor. Having given the thing the alien name, one may by a negative addition deny of it one of the attributes naturally associated with its new name. An instance of this would be to call the shield not the 'cup *of Ares*,' as in the former case, but a 'cup *that holds no wine*'. * * *

A coined word is a name which, being quite unknown among a people, is given by the composer himself; e.g. (for there are some words that seem to be of this origin) *'sprouters'* for horns, and *'pray-er'* for priest. A word is said to be lengthened out, when it has a short vowel made long, or an extra syllable inserted; e. g. *poleōs* for *poleōs*, *Pēlēiadeō* for *Pēleidou*. It is said to be curtailed, when it has lost a part; e.g. *kri*, *dō*, and *mia ginetai amphoterōn ops*. It is an altered word, when part is left as it was and part is of the composer's making; e.g. *dexiteron* for *dexion*, in *dexiteron kata maxon*.

The Nouns themselves (to whatever class they may

belong) are either masculines, feminines, or intermediates (neuter). All ending in N, P, S, or in the two compounds of this last, PS and X, are masculines. All ending in the invariably long vowels, H and Ō, and in A among the vowels that may be long, are feminines. So that there is an equal number of masculine and feminine terminations, as PS and X are the same as S, and need not be counted. There is no Noun, however, ending in a mute or in either of the two short vowels, E and O. Only three (*meli*, *kommi*, *peperi*) end in I, and five in U. The intermediates, or neuters, end in the variable vowels or in N, P, S.

Chapter 22

The perfection of speech is for it to be at once clear and not mean. The clearest indeed is that made up of the ordinary words for things, but it is mean, as is shown by the dramatic composition of Cleophon and Sthenelus. On the other hand the language becomes distinguished and non-prosaic by the use of unfamiliar terms, i.e. strange words, metaphors, lengthened forms, and everything that deviates from the ordinary modes of speech.

However, a whole statement in such terms will be either a riddle or a barbarism; a riddle, if made up of metaphors, a barbarism, if made up of strange words. The very nature indeed of a riddle is this, to describe a fact in an impossible combination of words (which cannot be done with the real names for things, but can be with their metaphorical substitutes); e.g. 'I saw a man glue brass on another with fire', and the like. The corresponding use of strange words results in a barbarism.

A certain admixture, accordingly, of unfamiliar terms is necessary. These, the strange word, the metaphor, the ornamental equivalent, etc. will save the language from seeming mean and prosaic, while the ordinary words in it will secure the requisite clearness. What helps most, however, to render the language at once clear and non-prosaic is the use of the lengthened, curtailed, and altered forms of words.

Their deviation from the ordinary words will, by making the language unlike that in general use give it a non-prosaic appearance; and their having much in common with the words in general use will give it the quality of clearness.

It is not right, then, to condemn these modes of speech, and ridicule the composer for using them, as some have done; e.g. the elder Euclid, who said it was easy to make dramatic composition if one were to be allowed to lengthen the words in the statement itself as much as one likes—a procedure he caricatured by reading *Epicharēn eidon Marathōnade badizonta* and *ouk an g' eramenos ton ekeinou elleboron* as verses. A too apparent use of these licences has certainly a ludicrous effect, but they are not alone in that; the rule of moderation applies to all the constituents of verse; even with metaphors, strange words, and the rest, the effect will be the same, if one uses them improperly and with a view to provoking laughter. The proper use of them is a very different thing.

To realize the difference one should take an epic verse and see how it reads when the normal words are introduced. The same should be done too with the strange word, the metaphor, and the rest; for one has only to put the ordinary words in their place to see the truth of what we are saying. The same iambic, for instance, is found in Aeschylus and Euripides, and as it stands in the former it is a poor line; whereas Euripides, by the change of a single word, the substitution of a strange for what is by usage the ordinary word, has made it seem a fine one.

Aeschylus having said in his *Philoctetes*:
　phagedainan hē mou sarkas esthiei podos
Euripides has merely altered the *esthiei* into *thoinatai*.

Or suppose
　nun de m' eōn oligos te kai outidanos kai aeikēs
to be altered by the substitution of the ordinary words into
　nun de m' eōn mikros te kai asthenikos kai aeikēs.

Or the line
　diphron aeikelion katatheis oligēn te trapezan
into

DRAMATICS

diphron mochthēron katatheis mikran te trapezan

Or *eiones booōsin* into *ēiones krazousin*.

Add to this that Ariphrades used to ridicule the tragedians for introducing expressions unknown in the language of common life, *dōmatōn apo* (for *apo dōmatōn*), *sethen*, *egō de nin*, *Achilleōs peri* (for *peri Achilleōs*), and the like. The mere fact of their not being in ordinary speech gives the language a non-prosaic character, but Ariphrades was unaware of that. It is a great thing, indeed, to make a proper use of these idiomatic forms, as also of compounds and strange words.

But the greatest thing by far is to be a master of metaphor. It is the one thing that cannot be learnt from others;[35] and it is also a sign of genius, since a good metaphor implies an intuitive perception of the similarity in dissimilars.

Of the kinds of words we have enumerated it may be observed that compounds are most in place in the dithyramb, strange words in heroic, and metaphors in iambics. Heroic composition, indeed, may avail itself of them all. But in iambic verse, which models itself as far as possible on the spoken language, only those

---

35 This is an extremely odd statement given that Aristotle has just spend one-half of Chapter 21 teaching the reader about metaphor. Did his views evolve and was Chapter 21 actually later?

kinds of words are in place which are allowable also in an oration, i.e. the ordinary word, the metaphor, and the ornamental equivalent.

Let this, then, suffice as an account of tragedy, the art representing by means of action on the stage.

Chapter 23

As for representation that merely narrates in versified language [without staged action], it is evident that it has several points in common with tragedy.

The construction of its plots should clearly be, just as in tragedy, dramatic;[36] they should be based on a single action, one that is a complete whole in itself, with a beginning, middle, and end, so as to enable the work to produce its own proper pleasure with all the organic unity of a living creature.

Nor should one suppose that there is anything like them in our usual histories. A history has to deal not with one action, but with one period and all that happened in that to one or more persons, however disconnected the several events may have been. Just as two events may take place at the same time, e.g. the sea-

---

36 Because epic is narrated, one way in which the plot as "combination of incidents" is different from that of tragedy, which is enacted by actors, is that the epic plot is imagined by the audience. As we see shortly, this leads to certain advantages over tragedy but also to disadvantages.

fight off Salamis and the battle with the Carthaginians in Sicily, without converging to the same end, so too of two consecutive events one may sometimes come after the other with no one end as their common issue. Nevertheless most of our epic composers, one may say, ignore the distinction.

Herein, then, to repeat what we have said before, we have a further proof of Homer's marvellous superiority to the rest. He did not attempt to deal even with the Trojan war in its entirety, though it was a whole with a definite beginning and end—through a feeling apparently that it was too long a story to be taken in in one view, or if not that, too complicated from the variety of incidents in it. As it is, he has singled out one section of the whole; many of the other incidents, however, he brings in as episodes, using the Catalogue of the Ships, for instance, and other episodes to relieve the uniformity of his narrative. As for the other epic composers, they treat of one man, or one period; or else of an action which, although one, has a multiplicity of parts in it. This last is what the authors of the *Cypria* and *Little Iliad* have done. And the result is that, whereas the *Iliad* or *Odyssey* supplies materials for only one, or at most two tragedies, the *Cypria* does that for several, and the *Little Iliad* for more than eight: for an *Adjudgment of Arms*, a *Philoctetes*, a *Neoptolemus*, a *Eurypylus*, a *Ulysses as Beggar*, a *Laconian Women*, a *Fall of Ilium*, and a *Departure of the Fleet*; as also a *Sinon*, and *Women of Troy*.

Chapter 24

Besides this, epic composition must divide into the same species as tragedy; it must be either simple or complex, a story of character or one of suffering. Its parts, too, with the exception of the music-dance [that is, primarily the singing and dancing chorus] and spectacle, must be the same, as it requires peripeties, discoveries, and scenes of suffering just like tragedy. Lastly, the thought and speech in it must be good in their way.

All these elements appear in Homer first; and he has made due use of them. His two works are constructed each [with the above-noted elements]: the *Iliad* simple and a story of suffering, the *Odyssey* complex (there is discovery throughout it) and a story of character. And they are more than this, since in language and thought too they surpass all other works. There is, however, a difference in epic as compared with tragedy, in its length and in its metre.

(1) As to its length, the limit already suggested [in Chapter 7] will suffice: it must be possible for the beginning and end of the work to be taken in in one view—a condition which will be fulfilled if the work be shorter than the old epics, and about as long as the series of tragedies offered for one hearing. For the extension of its length epic has a special advantage, of which it makes large use. *In a play one cannot represent an action with a number of parts going on*

simultaneously; one is limited to the part on the stage and connected with the actors. Whereas in epic the narrative form makes it possible for one to describe a number of simultaneous incidents; and these, if germane to the subject, increase the body of the composition. This then is a gain to the epic, tending to give it grandeur, and also variety of interest and room for episodes of diverse kinds. Uniformity of incident by the satiety it soon creates is apt to ruin tragedies on the stage.

(2) As for its metre, the heroic has been assigned it from experience; were any one to attempt a narrative work in some one, or in several, of the other metres, the incongruity of the thing would be apparent. The heroic in fact is the gravest and weightiest of metres—which is what makes it more tolerant than the rest of strange words and metaphors, that also being a point in which the narrative form of creation goes beyond all others. The iambic and trochaic tetrameter, on the other hand, are metres of movement, the one representing that of life and action, the other that of the dance. Still more unnatural would it appear, it one were to create an epic in a medley of metres, as Chaeremon did. Hence it is that no one has ever composed a long story in any but heroic verse; nature herself, as we have said, teaches us to select the metre appropriate to such a story.

Homer, admirable as he is in every other respect, is especially so in this, that he alone among epic-makers is not unaware of the part to be played by the composer himself in the work. The maker should say very little in his own person, as he is no imitator when doing that. Whereas the other composers are perpetually coming forward in person, and say but little, and that only here and there, as impersonators, Homer after a brief preface brings in forthwith [by impersonating them] a man, a woman, or some other character—no one of them characterless, but each with distinctive characteristics.

The marvellous is certainly required in tragedy. The epic, however, affords more opening for the improbable, the chief factor in the marvellous, because in it the agents are not visibly before one. The scene of the pursuit of Hector would be ridiculous on the stage—the Greeks halting instead of pursuing him, and Achilles shaking his head to stop them; but in the epic the absurdity is overlooked. The marvellous, however, is a cause of pleasure, as is shown by the fact that we all tell a story with additions, in the belief that we are doing our hearers a pleasure.

Homer more than any other has taught the rest of us the art of framing deceptions in the right way. I mean the use of paralogism. Whenever, if A is or happens, a consequent, B, is or happens, men's notion is that, if the B is, the A also is—but that is a false conclusion. Accordingly, if A is untrue, but there is something else, B, that on the assumption of its truth follows as its consequent, the right thing then is to add on the B. Just because we know the truth of the consequent, we are in our own minds led on to the erroneous inference of the truth of the antecedent. An instance is from the Bath-story in the *Odyssey*.

A likely impossibility is always preferable to an unconvincing possibility. The story should never be made up of improbable incidents; there should be nothing of the sort in it. If, however, such incidents are unavoidable, they should be outside the piece, like the hero's ignorance in *Oedipus* of the circumstances of Laius's death; not within it, like the report of the Pythian games in *Electra*, or the man's having come to Mysia from Tegea without uttering a word on the way, in *The Mysians*. So that it is ridiculous to say that one's plot would have been spoilt without them, since it is fundamentally wrong to make up such plots. If the composer has taken such a plot, however, and one sees that he might have put it in a more probable form, he is guilty of absurdity as well as a fault of art. Even in the *Odyssey* the improbabilities in the setting-ashore of Ulysses would be clearly intolerable in the hands of an inferior poet. As it is, the creator conceals them, his other excellences veiling their absurdity.

Elaborate speech, however, is required only in places where there is no action, and no character or thought to be revealed. Where there is character or thought, on the other hand, an over-ornate speech tends to obscure them.

Chapter 25 [37]

As regards Problems and their Solutions, one may see the number and nature of the assumptions on which they proceed by viewing the matter in the following way. (1) The composer being an imitator just like the painter or other maker of likenesses, he must necessarily in all instances represent things in one or other of three aspects, either as they were or are, or as they are said or thought to be or to have been, or as they ought to be. (2) All this he does in language, with an admixture, it may be, of strange words and metaphors, as also of the various modified forms of words, since the use of these is conceded in composition. (3) It is to be remembered, too, that there is not the same kind of correctness in the art of composition as in politics, or indeed any other art. There is, however, within the limits of [representational] composition itself a possibility of two kinds of error, the one directly, the other only accidentally connected with the art. If the composer meant to describe the thing correctly, and failed through lack of power of expression, his art itself is at fault. But if it was through his having meant to describe it in some incorrect way (e.g. to make the horse in movement have both right legs thrown forward) that the technical error (one in a matter of, say, medicine or some other special science), or impossibilities of whatever kind they may be, have got into his description, his error in that case is not in the

---

37 This chapter is often thought to have been originally part of the (mostly lost) *Homeric Problems*.

essentials of the compositional art.

These, therefore, must be the premisses of the Solutions in answer to the criticisms involved in the Problems.

I. As to the criticisms relating to the composer's art itself, any impossibilities there may be in his descriptions of things are faults. But from another point of view they are justifiable, if they serve the end of the art itself—if (to assume what we have said of that end) they make the effect of some portion of the work more astounding. The Pursuit of Hector is an instance in point. If, however, the end might have been as well or better attained without sacrifice of technical correctness in such matters, the impossibility is not to be justified, since the description should be, if it can, entirely free from error.

One may ask, too, whether the error is in a matter directly or only accidentally connected with the art; since it is a lesser error in an artist not to know, for instance, that the hind has no horns than to produce an unrecognizable picture of one.

II. If the composer's description be criticized as not true to fact, one may urge perhaps that the object ought to be as described—an answer like that of Sophocles, who said that he drew men as they ought to be, and Euripides as they were. If the description, however, be neither true nor of the thing as it ought to be, the answer must be then, that it is in accordance with opinion. The tales about Gods, for instance, may be as wrong as Xenophanes thinks, neither true nor the better thing to say; but they are certainly in accordance with opinion. Of other statements one may perhaps say, not that they are better than the truth, but that the fact was so at the time; e.g. the description of the arms: 'their spears stood upright, butt-end upon the ground'; for that was the usual way of fixing them then, as it is still with the Illyrians.

As for the question whether something said or done in a work is morally right or not, in dealing with that one should consider not only the intrinsic quality of the actual word or deed, but also the person who says or does it, the person to whom he says or does it, the time, the means, and the motive of the agent—whether he does it to attain a greater good or to avoid a greater evil.

III. Other criticisms one must meet by considering the language of the composer: (1) by the assumption of a strange word in a passage like *ouréas men prōton*, where by *ouréas* he [Homer] may mean not mules but sentinels. And in saying of Dolon, *hos p' ē toi eidos men eēn kakos*, his meaning may be, not that Dolon's body was deformed, but that his face was ugly, because *eueidos* is the Cretan word for handsome-faced.

So, too, *zōroteron de keraie* may mean not 'mix the wine stronger', as though for alcoholics, but 'mix it quicker'. (2) Other expressions in Homer may be explained as metaphorical; e.g. in *pantes men ra theoi te kai aneres hippokorustai eudon pannuchioi* as compared with what he tells us at the same time, *ē toi hot' es pedion to Trōikon athrēseien, aulōn suriggōn te homadon*, the word *pantes* 'all', is metaphorically put for 'many', since 'all' is a species of 'many'.

So also his *oiē d'ammoros* is metaphorical, the best known standing 'alone'. (3) A change, as Hippias of Thasos suggested, in the mode of reading a word will solve the difficulty in *didomen de hoi euchos aresthai* and *to men hou kataputhetai ombrō*. (4) Other difficulties may be solved by another punctuation; e.g. in Empedocles, *aipsa de thnēt' ephuonto, ta prin mathon athanat' einai zōra te prin kekrēto*. Or (5) by the assumption of an equivocal term, as in *parōchēken de pleō nux*, where *pleiō* in equivocal. Or (6) by an appeal to the custom of language. Wine-and-water we call 'wine'; and it is on the same principle that Homer speaks of a *knēmis neoteuktou kassiteroio*, a 'greave of new-wrought tin'. A worker in iron we call a 'brazier'; and it is on the same principle that Ganymede is described as the 'wine-server' of Zeus, though the Gods do not drink wine.

This latter, however, may be an instance of metaphor. But whenever also a word seems to imply some contradiction, it is necessary to reflect how many ways there may be of understanding it in the passage in question; e.g. in Homer's *tē r' escheto chalkeon egchos* one should consider the possible senses of 'was stopped there'—whether, by taking it in this sense or in that, one will best avoid the fault of which Glaucon speaks:

> They start with some improbable presumption; and having so decreed it themselves, proceed to draw inferences, and censure the composer as though he had actually said whatever they happen to believe, if his statement conflicts with their own notion of things.

This is how Homer's silence about Icarius has been treated. Starting with the notion of his having been a Lacedaemonian [i.e., Spartan], the critics think it strange for Telemachus not to have met him when he went to Lacedaemon. Whereas the fact may have been as the Cephallenians say, that the wife of Ulysses was of a Cephallenian family, and that her father's name was Icadius, not Icarius. So that it is probably a mistake of the critics that has given rise to the Problem.

Speaking generally, one has to justify (1) the Impossible by reference to the requirements of [artistic] composition, or to the better, or to opinion. For the purposes of composition, a convincing impossibility is preferable to an unconvincing possibility; and if men such as Zeuxis depicted be impossible, the answer is that it is better they should be like that, as the artist ought to improve on his model. (2) The Improbable one has to justify either by showing it to be in accordance with opinion, or by urging that at times it is not improbable; for there is a probability of things happening also against probability. (3) The contradictions found in the composer's language one should first test as one does an opponent's confutation in a dialectical argument, so as to see whether he means the same thing, in the same relation, and in the same sense, before admitting that he has contradicted either something he has said himself or what a man of sound sense assumes as true. But there is no possible apology for improbability of plot or depravity of character, when they are not necessary and no use is made of them, like the improbability in the appearance of Aegeus in *Medea* and the baseness of Menelaus in *Orestes*.

The objections, then, of critics start with faults of five kinds: the allegation is always that something is either (1) impossible, (2) improbable, (3) corrupting, (4) contradictory, or (5) against technical correctness. The answers to these objections must be sought under one or other of the above-mentioned heads, which are twelve in number.

Chapter 26

The question may be raised whether epic or tragedy is the higher form of representation. It may be argued that, if the less vulgar is the higher and the less vulgar is always that which addresses the better public, an art addressing any and every one is of a very vulgar order. It is a belief that their public cannot see the meaning, unless they add something themselves, that causes the perpetual movements of the performers—bad double-oboe players, for instance, rolling about, if discus-throwing is to be represented, and pulling at the choral leader, if Scylla is the subject of the piece.[38]

Tragedy, then, is said to be an art of this order—to be in fact just what the later actors were in the eyes of their predecessors; for Mynniscus used to call Callippides 'the ape', because he thought he so overacted his parts; and a similar view was taken of Pindarus also. All tragedy, however, is said to stand to epic as the newer to the older school of actors. The one, accordingly, is said to address a cultivated audience, which does not need the accompaniment of gesture; the other, an uncultivated one. If, therefore, tragedy is a vulgar art, it must clearly be lower than the epic.[39]

The answer to this is twofold. In the first place, one may urge (i) that the censure does not touch the art of the dramatist, but only that of his interpreter; *for it is quite possible to overdo the gesturing even in an epic recital, as did Sosistratus, and in a singing contest, as did Mnasitheus of Opus.* (ii) That one should not condemn all movement, unless one means to condemn even the dance, but only that of ignoble people—which

---

38 Scylla was a legendary monster who resided on one side of a very narrow strait of water, with the whirlpool Charybdis on the other side. Sailors had to "thread the needle" or perish. Hence the saying "between Scylla and Charybdis."

39 Aristotle is probably addressing the Platonists, because Plato ranks epic highest at *Laws* II, 658d and at *Republic* 394c, 397d and 398d. See *ADMC*, p. 165.

is the point of the criticism passed on Callippides and in the present day on others, that their women are not like gentlewomen. (iii) That tragedy may produce its effect even without movement or action in just the same way as epic; for from the mere reading of a play its quality may be seen. So that, if it be superior in all other respects, this element of inferiority is not a necessary part of it.

In the second place, one must remember (i) that tragedy has everything that epic has (even the epic metre being admissible), together with a not inconsiderable addition in the shape of the music-dance (a very real factor in the pleasure of the drama) and the spectacle. (ii) That its reality of presentation is felt in the play as read, as well as in the play as acted. (iii) That the impersonation of tragedy requires less space for the attainment of its end; which is a great advantage, since the more concentrated effect is more pleasurable than one with a large admixture of time to dilute it— consider the *Oedipus* of Sophocles, for instance, and the effect of expanding it into the number of lines of the *Iliad*. (iv) That there is less unity in the representation of the epic-makers, as is proved by the fact that any one work of theirs supplies matter for several tragedies; the result being that, if they take what is really a single story, it seems curt when briefly told, and thin and waterish when on the scale of length usual with their verse. In saying that there is less unity in an epic, I mean an epic made up of a plurality of actions, in the same way as the *Iliad* and *Odyssey* have many such parts, each one of them in itself of some magnitude; yet the structure of the two Homeric creations is as perfect as can be, and the action in them is as nearly as possible one action.

If, then, tragedy is superior in these respects, and also besides these, in its artistic function (since the two creative forms should give us, not any or every pleasure, but the very special kind we have mentioned[40]), it is clear that, as attaining the end better than epic, it will be the higher form of art.

So much for tragedy and epic—for these two arts in general and their species; the number and nature of their constituent parts; the causes of success and failure in them; the objections of the critics, and the solutions in answer to them.[41]

---

40 It is easier to consider that the passage explaining this "special pleasure" is lost than to refer back to an extant passage. For instance, the pleasure of imitations in Chapter 4 also includes painting, and it would be very debatable whether this kind of pleasure is therefore properly "special."

41 Leaving aside that at least one manuscript has words showing that Aristotle subsequently fulfills his promise in Chapter 6 to discuss comedy, a discussion that is lost, we might consider how the Northern Greek has closed the circle, beginning with the very first sentence in the treatise, in which he promises to consider the species, parts and how to succeed. Objections of critics and the solutions to them were never mentioned there, in Chapter 1. It is as if a later editor, once interpolating Chapter 25, felt it was necessary to add the additional theme from that chapter, namely, objections and the solutions, as he closes out the extant treatise.

Bibliography

Aristotle

Bywater, Ingram. *On the Art of Poetry*, with a Preface by Gilbert Murray (Oxford: Clarendon Press, 1920).

The Complete Works of Aristotle: The Revised Oxford Translation, ed. Jonathan Barnes (Princeton: Princeton University Press, 1984).

The Works of Aristotle, Vol. II, *Problemata*, by E.F. Forster, under the editorship of W.D. Ross (Oxford: Clarendon Press, 1930).

Aristotle in 23 Volumes, Vol. 23, translated by W.H. Fyfe (Cambridge, MA, Harvard University Press; London, William Heinemann Ltd., 1932). Also at—
   http://www.perseus.tufts.edu/hopper/text?doc=Perseus:text:1999.01.0056

Tarán, Leonardo and Dimitri Gutas. *Aristotle Poetics: Editio Maior of the Greek Text with Historical Introduction and Philological Commentaries* (Brill: Leiden and Boston, 2012).

Costelloe, B.F.C. and J.H. Muirhead, *Aristotle and the Earlier Peripatetics: Being a Translation from Zeller's "Philosophy of the Greeks,"* in Two Volumes (New York: Russell & Russell, Inc., 1962).

Halliwell, Stephen. *Aristotle's Poetics* (Chapel Hill and London: The University of North Carolina Press, 1986).
---. *Between Ecstasy and Truth* (Oxford: Oxford University Press, 2011).

Janko, Richard. *Aristotle: Poetics, with the Tractatus Coisilianus, Reconstruction of Poetics II, and the Fragments of the On Poets* (Indianapolis: Hackett Publishing Company, 1987).
---. Book review of Tarán and Gutas, *Classical Philology* 108 (2013) 252–7, also at: http://www-personal.umich.edu/~rjanko/review%20Gutas%20&%20Tar%E1n.pdf

Natali, Carlo. *Aristotle: His Life and School*, ed. by D.S. Hutchinson (Princeton: Princeton University Press, 2013).

Notomi, Noburu. "Image-Making in *Republic* X and the *Sophist*," in *Plato and the Poets*, ed. by P. Destrée and F. Herrmann (Leiden & Boston: Brill, 2011) 299-326.

Scott, Gregory L. "The *Poetics* of Performance: The Necessity of Performance, Spectacle, Music, and Dance in Aristotelian Tragedy," in *Performance and Authenticity in the Arts (Cambridge Series on Philosophy and the Arts)* eds. Salim Kemal and Ivan Gaskell (Cambridge: Cambridge University Press, 1999) 15-48.
---. "Purging the *Poetics*," *Oxford Studies in Ancient*

Philosophy, Vol. 25 (Winter 2003) 233-264.

---. *Aristotle's Favorite Tragedy: Oedipus or Cresphontes?* (New York: ExistencePS Press, 2nd ed. 2018; orig. publ. 2016).

---. *Aristotle on Dramatic Musical Composition: The Real Role of Literature, Catharsis, Music and Dance in the POETICS* (New York: ExistencePS Press, 2nd ed., 2018; originally published 2016). (Abbreviated often as *ADMC*.)

---. *A Primer on Aristotle's DRAMATICS (also known as the POETICS)* (New York: ExistencePS Press, 2019).

Veloso, Claudio William, with a Preface by Marwan Rashed. *Pourquoi la Poétique d'Aristote? DIAGOGÈ* (Paris: Vrin, 2018).

Zeller, Eduard. See Costelloe.

Biography
Gregory L. Scott

Scott finished his PhD at the University of Toronto (Philosophy) under the supervision of Francis Sparshott. Subsequently, he taught full-time in philosophy departments in the USA and Canada. He was also a Visiting Research Fellow/Scholar at Princeton University, Philosophy (sponsor: Sarah Broadie) and the University of Texas, Austin, Philosophy (sponsor: Alexander Mourelatos).

Insights from Aristotle's use of "possibility" in the *Dramatics* helped give Scott the intuitions for *Aristotle's "Not to Fear" Proof for the Necessary Eternality of the Universe* (2019), which explains how and why the Stagirite gave up his youthful doctrine of the Unmoved Mover, often called God, of *Metaphysics* Lambda, in favor of a proof for the *necessary* eternality of the universe. The proof depends solely on the infinite past and a profound understanding of the modals "necessity," "possibility," and "impossibility." The book also explains why none of the later philosophers, either in or out of the Peripatos, for at least 300 years paid attention to the Unmoved Mover, until Andronicus of Rhodes (1st century BCE) and especially Alexander of Aphrodisias (in the 3rd century CE) assumed wrongly that it was part of the mature corpus and, at least on Alexander's part, tried to make sense of it, a frustration that has continued to this day for theologians.

Having a background in ballet, with training at the San Francisco Ballet School and teacher training at the National Ballet School of Canada, and having published in scholarly dance journals, Scott also directed the doctoral program in Dance Education at New York University. He is currently writing a book on the philosophy of Western theatrical dance and is developing a new theory of dance composition called "melkines," which are to dance as melodies are to music.

www.ingramcontent.com/pod-product-compliance
Lightning Source LLC
Chambersburg PA
CBHW072038110526
44592CB00012B/1467